CW00346191

GI & GL
counter

Dr Wynnie Chan

Bounty
Books

First published in Great Britain in 2006 by Hamlyn,
a division of Octopus Publishing Group Ltd

This edition published 2007 by Bounty Books,
a division of Octopus Publishing Group Ltd,
2–4 Heron Quays, London E14 4JP

ISBN-13: 978-0-7537-1514-7
ISBN-10: 0-7537-1514-7

A CIP catalogue record for this book is available
from the British Library

Printed and bound in China

Nutrient information has been calculated using data from the
UK Food Nutrient Databank which is available from The Food
Standards Agency (FSA). Some values have been estimated
based on similar foods.

The information in this book is intended only as a guide
to following a healthy diet. People with special dietary
requirements of any kind should consult appropriate
medical professionals before changing their diet.

CONTENTS

What are GI and GL?

Glycaemic Index

The glycaemic index (GI) is a measure of the ability of a food to raise blood glucose (sugar) levels after it has been eaten. The GI of a food is determined by several factors such as how much it's been processed, what type of cooking method has been used and the presence of nutrients such as protein and fat.

How does it work?

When glucose is released into the bloodstream during digestion, our body produces a hormone called insulin whose function is to transport glucose to places where it is needed for fuel – usually the muscle cells and the brain.

While our bodies can handle a steady release of glucose during digestion, when large quantities flood the bloodstream, the body's regulatory system goes into overload and produces large amounts of insulin to clear the glucose away into the body cells. This surge in insulin has the unfortunate effect of heightening our feelings of hunger which in turn increases our desire to eat more carbs.

Regrettably excess carbs get stored away in our fat cells. If this happens frequently, it can lead to weight gain and over time can even damage our cells by causing insulin resistance in which cells that normally respond to insulin become less sensitive to its effects.

Insulin resistance, high insulin levels and excess high GI foods have all been linked with Type II or middle-aged onset diabetes as well as premature ageing, heart disease and some cancers.

The benefits of eating low GI foods

Health experts believe that eating foods which cause a slow and steady rise of blood sugar levels, known as low GI foods, can have advantages for those watching their waistlines as well as for diabetic patients. This is because low GI foods help to delay feelings of hunger, compared to high GI foods thus helping you to control your calorie intake.

There are a number of scientific studies that show that people who eat low GI foods lose more body fat than those who eat high GI foods.

Glycaemic Load

The Glycaemic Load (GL) is a related measure and is calculated by multiplying the GI of a food by the amount of carbohydrate per typical serving and dividing it by 100.

GL is more reliable than the glycaemic index as a predictor of how a food will affect the blood sugar level. This is because some foods which have a high GI like carrots or watermelon contain such a small amount of carbohydrate in a normal portion that they would not be expected to raise the blood sugar levels very much. On the other hand, watermelon or carrot juice contains a larger amount of carbohydrate which would cause a larger increase in blood sugar levels.

Glycaemic Load can be calculated using the following equation:

$$GL = \frac{GI \times carbohydrate\ per\ portion}{100}$$

New evidence is emerging that links high GL meals with an increased risk for heart disease and diabetes, especially in overweight and insulin-resistant people.

Understanding GI and GL ratings

- **Low GI and low GL** A food that has a low glycaemic load will have a small effect on blood glucose levels, as it either doesn't contain a lot of carbohydrate and/or it has a low GI score.
- **Low GI and high GL** Even low GI foods, if eaten in large quantities, can affect (raise) blood glucose levels quite significantly, especially if they are concentrated sources of carbohydrates (for example, most cakes, dried fruit and dried fruit bars, fruit juices and crisps).
- **High GI and low GL** These foods contain a small amount of carbohydrate in typical serving sizes and will not affect blood glucose levels significantly even though they have a high GI. It is important to remember that these should not be eaten with other high GI or high GL foods.
- **High GI and high GL** These foods will cause a dramatic increase in blood glucose levels and so should be avoided wherever possible.

Healthy eating

Whether you want to lose just a few kilograms or rather more, eating healthily is vital. This does not mean cutting out all of your favourite treats completely, just eating them in moderation. If you're not enjoying your food, you are less likely to stick to your diet and exercise regime.

Losing weight doesn't just mean that you'll have more energy and will feel better about yourself, it also decreases the risk of developing various ailments, including diabetes, hypertension, coronary heart disease, stroke, respiratory problems, gallstones and some cancers.

A balanced diet

Including foods from the five food groups means that you are meeting your requirements for nutrients.

THE FIVE GROUPS ARE:

1 Bread, cereals and potatoes This group is rich in starchy carbohydrates and includes breakfast cereals, rice, pasta, noodles, yams and oats and should form the basis of most meals. Foods in this group are rich in insoluble fibre, calcium, iron and B vitamins, which are needed to keep your gut, bones and blood healthy. Try to eat wholegrain, wholemeal or high-fibre versions of breads and cereals.

2 Fruits and vegetables These are important sources of antioxidants such as vitamin C and beta-carotene (vegetable vitamin A), which protect us from cancers and heart disease. They are also rich in soluble fibre, which helps lower blood cholesterol. Try to include five portions of different fruits and vegetables in your diet each day, whether fresh, frozen, canned, dried or juiced.

3 Milk and dairy foods These are excellent sources of calcium, protein and vitamins A and B12, and are essential for maintaining the health of bones, skin and blood. Include a couple of reduced-fat servings from this food group each day.

4 Meat, fish and alternatives The main nutrients supplied by this food group include iron, protein, B vitamins, zinc and magnesium, which help to maintain healthy blood and an efficient immune system. Choose at most two servings of lean red meat, fish, chicken, nuts, turkey, eggs, beans or pulses. The last two are great protein alternatives, as is tofu, which is also a good source of calcium.

5 Foods containing sugar or fat Minimize your intake of savoury snacks, biscuits, cakes, crisps, pastries, sweets, chocolate, pies, butter and carbonated drinks, as these will hinder your efforts to lose weight.

How to use this book

This book lists the GI and GL rating, energy – as kilocalories (kcal) and kilojoules (kJ) – fat, saturated fat, protein, carbohydrate and fibre contained in more than 1,500 foods. Nutrient values have been expressed as average servings so no calculator is needed.

The information shows where the energy comes from in any food so, if you're on a low-carbohydrate, low-fat diet or have any other special requirements, you can work out exactly how much you can have of any food.

Guideline Daily Amounts

Guideline Daily Amounts (GDAs) are daily guideline figures recommended by health professionals for intake of calories, fat and saturates for adult women and men. These are average figures and personal requirements will vary with age, weight and levels of activity.

AVERAGE DAILY REQUIREMENT

	women	men
kcal	2000	2500
fat	70g	95g
saturates	20g	30g

Dietary Reference Values

Dietary Reference Values (DRVs) are daily recommendations set by the Department of Health for the nutrients considered sufficient for most adults and children in the UK. The table below gives the average daily requirement for protein, carbohydrate and fibre. If you are trying to lose weight, you will need less, and should discuss the exact amounts with your doctor or dietician.

AVERAGE DAILY REQUIREMENT

	women	men
protein	46g	56g
carbohydrate	225g	300g
fibre	18g	18g

GI and GL ratings

Each food has been assigned a low, medium or high GI and a low, medium or high GL rating. The ratings are:

H = high
M = medium
L = low

FRUITS	AVERAGE PORTION g	GI	GL
Apples, cooking	130	L	L
Apples, cooking, stewed with sugar	110	M	M
Apples, cooking, stewed without sugar	85	L	L
Apples, Cox's Pippin	100	L	L
Apples, Golden Delicious	100	L	L
Apples, Granny Smith	100	L	L
Apples, red dessert	100	L	L
Apricots	80	M	M
Apricots, canned in juice	140	M	M
Apricots, dried	120	L	L
Apricots, stewed with sugar	140	M	M
Apricots, stewed without sugar	140	L	L
Avocado, Fuerte	173	L	L
Avocado, Hass	173	L	L
Avocado (small)	100	L	L
Banana chips	13	M	H
Bananas	100	L	H
Bilberries	40	L	L
Blackberries	100	L	L
Blackberries, stewed with sugar	140	M	M
Blackberries, stewed without sugar	140	L	L
Blackcurrants	100	L	L
Blackcurrants, canned in juice	140	M	M
Blackcurrants, canned in syrup	140	M	M
Blackcurrants, stewed with sugar	140	M	M
Blackcurrants, stewed without sugar	140	L	L
Blueberries, raw	68	L	L
Carambola	120	L	L
Cherries	80	L	L
Cherries, canned in syrup	68	M	M
Cherries, glacé	15	M	M
Clementines	60	L	L
Cranberries	75	L	L
Currants	25	H	H

Unless otherwise stated, fruits are prepared but uncooked.

ENERGY kcal	ENERGY kJ	FAT g	SATURATED FAT g	PROTEIN g	CARBO-HYDRATE g	FIBRE g
46	196	Trace	Trace	0	12	2.1
81	345	Trace	Trace	0	21	1.3
28	117	Trace	Trace	0	7	1.3
46	195	Trace	Trace	1	11	2
43	185	Trace	Trace	0	11	1.7
45	193	Trace	Trace	0	12	1.7
51	217	Trace	Trace	0	13	1.9
25	107	Trace	Trace	1	6	1.4
48	206	Trace	Trace	1	12	1.3
190	809	1	Trace	5	44	7.6
101	431	Trace	Trace	1	26	2.2
38	161	Trace	Trace	1	9	2.1
327	1349	33	6.1	4	3	5.9
330	1362	34	8.1	3	3	5.9
190	784	20	4.1	1.9	1.9	3.4
66	278	4	Trace	0	8	0.2
95	403	1	0.1	1	23	1.1
12	51	Trace	Trace	0	3	0.7
25	104	Trace	Trace	1	5	3.1
78	335	Trace	Trace	1	19	3.4
29	123	Trace	Trace	1	6	3.6
28	121	Trace	Trace	1	7	3.6
43	189	Trace	Trace	1	11	4.3
101	428	Trace	Trace	1	26	3.6
81	353	Trace	Trace	1	21	3.9
34	144	Trace	Trace	1	8	4.3
38	159	0	0	0.5	9.6	1.7
38	163	1	0.1	1	9	1.6
38	162	Trace	Trace	1	9	0.7
48	207	Trace	Trace	0	13	0.4
39	159	Trace	Trace	0	9	0
22	95	Trace	Trace	1	5	0.7
11	49	Trace	Trace	0	3	2.3
67	285	Trace	Trace	1	17	0.5

FRUITS	AVERAGE PORTION g	GI	GL
Custard apples	60	L	L
Damsons	80	L	L
Damsons, stewed with sugar	100	M	M
Damsons, stewed without sugar	100	L	L
Dates	100	H	H
Dates, stoned and dried	60	H	H
Durian	80	L	L
Figs	55	L	L
Figs, dried	84	H	H
Fruit cocktail, canned in juice	115	L	M
Fruit cocktail, canned in syrup	115	M	L
Fruit salad, mixed	140	L	L
Gooseberries	100	L	L
Gooseberries, canned in syrup	140	M	M
Gooseberries, stewed with sugar	140	M	M
Gooseberries, stewed without sugar	140	L	L
Grapefruit	231	L	L
Grapefruit, canned in juice	120	L	L
Grapefruit, canned in syrup	120	M	M
Grapes	100	L	L
Greengages	100	L	L
Greengages, stewed with sugar	100	M	M
Greengages, stewed without sugar	100	L	L
Guavas	100	L	L
Guavas, canned in syrup	113	M	M
Kiwi fruit	60	L	L
Kumquats	8	L	L
Kumquats, canned in syrup	8	M	M
Lemons, unpeeled	60	L	L
Limes, unpeeled	40	L	L
Loganberries, canned in juice	140	L	L
Loganberries, stewed with sugar	140	M	M
Loganberries, stewed without sugar	140	L	L
Lychees	90	L	L

Unless otherwise stated, fruits are prepared but uncooked.

ENERGY kcal	ENERGY kJ	FAT g	SATURATED FAT g	PROTEIN g	CARBOHYDRATE g	FIBRE g
41	178	Trace	Trace	1	10	1.4
30	130	Trace	Trace	0	8	1.4
74	316	Trace	Trace	0	19	1.5
34	147	Trace	Trace	1	9	1.6
124	530	Trace	Trace	2	31	1.8
162	691	1	0.1	2	41	2.4
109	460	1	Trace	2	23	3
24	102	1	0.1	1	5	0.8
176	747	1	Trace	3	41	5.8
33	140	Trace	Trace	0	8	1.2
66	281	Trace	Trace	0	17	1.2
77	332	Trace	Trace	1	19	2.1
40	170	1	0.1	1	9	2.4
102	434	Trace	Trace	1	26	2.4
76	321	Trace	Trace	1	18	2.7
22	92	Trace	Trace	1	4	2.8
69	291	Trace	Trace	2	16	3
36	144	Trace	Trace	1	9	0.5
72	308	Trace	Trace	1	19	0.7
60	257	Trace	Trace	0	15	0.7
41	173	Trace	Trace	1	10	2.1
81	347	Trace	Trace	1	21	1.9
36	155	Trace	Trace	1	9	1.9
26	112	1	Trace	1	5	3.7
68	292	Trace	Trace	0	18	3.4
29	124	Trace	Trace	1	6	1.1
3	15	Trace	Trace	0	1	0.3
11	46	Trace	Trace	0	3	0.1
8	36	1	0.1	0	1	1.7
4	14	0	0	0	0	1.1
141	601	Trace	Trace	1	37	2.2
70	300	Trace	Trace	1	18	2.8
20	87	Trace	Trace	1	4	2.9
52	223	Trace	Trace	1	13	0.6

FRUITS	AVERAGE PORTION g	GI	GL
Lychees, canned in syrup	80	M	H
Mandarin oranges (medium)	70	L	L
Mandarin oranges, canned in juice	115	L	L
Mandarin oranges, canned in syrup	126	L	M
Mangoes, ripe	150	L	L
Mangoes, canned in syrup	105	M	L
Mangosteen	60	L	L
Melon, Canteloupe	150	H	H
Melon, Galia	150	H	H
Melon, Honeydew	200	H	H
Mixed peel	5	H	L
Nectarines	150	L	L
Oranges	160	L	L
Papaya	140	M	L
Passion fruit	60	L	L
Peaches	110	L	L
Peaches, canned in juice	120	L	L
Peaches, canned in syrup	120	M	M
Pears, canned in juice	135	L	L
Pears, canned in syrup	135	M	M
Pears, Comice	150	L	L
Pears, Conference	170	M	M
Pears, Nashi	150	L	L
Pears, William	150	L	L
Physalis	60	L	L
Pineapple	80	M	L
Pineapple, canned in juice	40	L	L
Pineapple, canned in syrup	40	M	M
Plums, average, stewed with sugar	133	M	M
Plums, average, stewed without sugar	70	L	L
Plums, canned in syrup	80	M	M
Plums, Victoria	55	L	L
Plums, yellow, raw	55	L	L
Pomegranate	55	L	L

Unless otherwise stated, fruits are prepared but uncooked.

ENERGY kcal	ENERGY kJ	FAT g	SATURATED FAT g	PROTEIN g	CARBO- HYDRATE g	FIBRE g
54	232	Trace	Trace	0	14	0.4
25	103	0	0	0.6	5.6	1
37	155	Trace	Trace	0.8	8.9	0.3
66	281	Trace	Trace	0.6	16.9	0.3
86	368	1	0.2	1	21	3.9
81	347	Trace	Trace	0	21	0.7
44	184	Trace	Trace	0	10	1
29	122	Trace	Trace	1	6	1.5
36	153	Trace	Trace	1	8	0.6
56	238	Trace	Trace	1	13	1.2
12	49	Trace	Trace	0	3	0.2
60	257	Trace	Trace	2	14	1.8
59	253	Trace	Trace	2	14	2.7
50	214	Trace	Trace	1	12	3.1
22	91	1	0.1	2	3	2
36	156	Trace	Trace	1	8	1.7
47	198	Trace	Trace	1	12	1
66	280	Trace	Trace	1	17	1.1
45	190	Trace	Trace	0	11	1.9
68	290	Trace	Trace	0	18	1.5
50	212	Trace	Trace	0	13	3
90	386	1	Trace	1	22	4.1
44	183	Trace	Trace	0	11	2.3
51	215	Trace	Trace	1	12	3.3
32	131	Trace	Trace	1	7	1
33	141	Trace	Trace	0	8	1
19	80	Trace	Trace	0	5	0.2
26	109	Trace	Trace	0	7	0.3
105	446	Trace	Trace	1	27	1.7
21	90	Trace	Trace	0	5	0.9
47	202	Trace	Trace	0	12	0.6
21	92	Trace	Trace	0	5	1
14	59	0	Trace	0.3	3.2	0.6
28	120	Trace	Trace	1	6	1.9

FRUITS	AVERAGE PORTION g	GI	GL
Pomelo	80	L	L
Prickly pears	60	L	L
Prunes, canned in juice	24	L	L
Prunes, canned in syrup	24	L	L
Prunes, dried	66	M	L
Prunes, stewed with sugar	24	M	M
Prunes, stewed without sugar	24	L	L
Quinces	90	L	L
Raisins	30	M	H
Rambutan	80	L	L
Raspberries	60	L	L
Raspberries, canned in syrup	90	M	M
Raspberries, stewed with sugar	90	M	M
Raspberries, stewed without sugar	90	L	L
Redcurrants	2	L	L
Redcurrants, stewed with sugar	140	M	M
Redcurrants, stewed without sugar	140	L	L
Rhubarb, canned in syrup	140	L	L
Rhubarb, stewed with sugar	140	M	M
Rhubarb, stewed without sugar	140	L	L
Satsumas	70	L	L
Sharon fruit	110	M	L
Starfruit	120	L	L
Strawberries	100	L	L
Sugar apples	60	L	L
Sultanas	18	M	H
Tangerines	70	L	L
Watermelon	200	H	H

Unless otherwise stated, fruits are prepared but uncooked.

ENERGY kcal	ENERGY kJ	FAT g	SATURATED FAT g	PROTEIN g	CARBO- HYDRATE g	FIBRE g
24	101	Trace	Trace	0	5	0.8
29	124	1	0.1	0	7	2.2
19	80	Trace	Trace	0	5	0.6
22	93	Trace	Trace	0	6	0.7
93	397	Trace	Trace	2	22	3.8
25	105	Trace	Trace	0	6	0.7
19	83	Trace	0	0	5	0.8
23	99	Trace	Trace	0	6	1.7
82	348	Trace	Trace	1	21	0.6
55	234	Trace	Trace	1	13	0.5
15	65	1	0.1	1	3	1.5
79	337	Trace	Trace	1	20	1.4
57	244	1	0.1	1	14	2
22	95	1	0.1	1	4	2.2
0	2	Trace	Trace	0	0	0.1
74	318	Trace	Trace	1	19	3.8
24	106	Trace	Trace	1	5	4.1
43	182	Trace	Trace	1	11	1.1
67	284	Trace	Trace	1	16	1.7
10	42	Trace	Trace	1	1	1.8
25	109	Trace	Trace	1	6	0.9
80	342	Trace	Trace	1	20	1.8
38	163	1	0.1	1	9	1.6
27	113	Trace	Trace	1	6	1.1
41	178	Trace	Trace	1	10	1.4
50	211	Trace	Trace	0	12	0.4
25	103	Trace	Trace	1	6	0.9
62	266	1	0.2	1	14	0.2

VEGETABLES	AVERAGE PORTION g	GI	GL
Ackee, canned	80	L	L
Alfalfa sprouts	5	L	L
Artichoke, globe, heart	40	L	L
Artichoke, Jerusalem	56	M	L
Asparagus	125	L	L
Aubergine, raw (half)	100	L	L
Aubergine, fried	130	L	L
Bamboo shoots, canned	50	L	L
Beans			
Aduki, dried, boiled	60	L	L
Baked, canned in tomato sauce	135	M	M
Baked, canned in tomato sauce, reduced sugar and salt	135	M	M
Baked, canned in tomato sauce, with burgers	225	M	M
Baked, canned in tomato sauce, with pork sausages	225	M	M
Balor, canned	135	L	L
Barbecue, canned in sauce	135	M	M
Blackeye, canned	55	L	L
Blackeye, dried, boiled	60	L	M
Broad	120	H	L
Broad, canned	120	H	L
Broad, frozen	120	H	L
Butter, canned	120	L	L
Butter, dried, boiled	60	L	L
Chickpeas, canned	70	L	L
Chickpeas, split, dried, boiled	70	L	L
Chickpeas, whole, dried, boiled	70	L	L
Chilli, canned	135	L	L
French	90	L	L
French, canned	90	L	L
French, frozen	90	L	L
Green	90	L	L

Unless otherwise stated, vegetables are described as they would normally be eaten.

ENERGY kcal	ENERGY kJ	FAT g	SATURATED FAT g	PROTEIN g	CARBO-HYDRATE g	FIBRE g
121	500	12	Trace	2	1	1.4
1	5	Trace	Trace	0	0	0.1
7	31	0	0	1	1	2
23	116	Trace	Trace	1	6	2
33	138	1	0.1	4	2	1.7
15	64	0	0	0.9	2.2	2
393	1620	41	5.3	2	4	3
6	23	1	0.1	1	0	0.9
74	315	Trace	Trace	6	14	3.3
109	466	1	0.1	6	20	4.7
99	420	1	0.1	7	17	5.1
214	900	7	0.1	15	25	6.8
239	1001	10	0.1	14	25	6.3
26	112	Trace	Trace	3	4	3.6
104	444	1	0.1	7	19	4.7
149	623	1	0	10	28	10
70	296	1	0.1	5	12	2.1
58	245	1	0.1	6	7	6.5
104	444	1	0.1	10	15	6.2
97	413	1	0.1	9	14	7.8
92	392	1	0.1	7	16	5.5
62	262	1	0.1	4	11	3.1
81	341	2	0.2	5	11	2.9
80	339	1	0.1	5	12	3
85	358	1	0.1	6	13	3
95	513	1	0.1	7	16	5.3
20	83	1	0.1	2	3	2.2
20	86	Trace	Trace	1	4	2.3
23	97	Trace	Trace	2	4	3.7
20	83	1	0.1	2	3	2.2

VEGETABLES	AVERAGE PORTION g	GI	GL
Green, canned	90	L	L
Green, frozen	90	L	L
Haricot, dried, boiled	60	L	M
Kidney, cooked	60	L	M
Kidney, dried	60	L	L
Lilva, canned	80	L	L
Mung, dahl, dried, boiled	60	L	L
Mung, whole, dried, boiled	60	L	L
Papri, canned	60	L	L
Pigeon peas, dahl, dried	60	L	L
Pinto, dried, boiled	60	L	L
Pinto, refried	60	L	L
Red kidney, canned	60	L	L
Red kidney, dried, boiled	60	L	L
Runner	90	L	L
Soya, dried, boiled	60	L	L
Beansprouts, mung	80	L	L
Beansprouts, mung, canned	80	L	L
Beansprouts, mung, stir-fried	80	L	L
Beetroot	40	M	L
Beetroot, pickled	35	M	L
Breadfruit, canned	40	L	L
Broccoli, green	85	L	L
Broccoli, purple sprouting	85	L	L
Brussels sprouts, steamed	90	L	L
Cabbage, Chinese	40	L	L
Cabbage, red	90	L	L
Cabbage, red, raw	90	L	L
Cabbage, Savoy	95	L	L
Cabbage, white	95	L	L
Cabbage, white, raw	90	L	L
Carrots, canned	60	M	L
Carrots, old	60	M	L
Carrots, old, raw	80	M	L

Unless otherwise stated, vegetables are described as they would normally be eaten.

ENERGY kcal	ENERGY kJ	FAT g	SATURATED FAT g	PROTEIN g	CARBO-HYDRATE g	FIBRE g
20	86	Trace	Trace	1	4	2.3
23	97	Trace	Trace	2	4	3.7
57	244	1	0.1	4	10	3.7
62	264	0	0.1	5	10.4	4
60	254	0	0.1	4.1	10.7	3.7
54	232	1	0.1	5	8	0.5
55	235	1	0.1	5	9	1.8
55	233	1	0.1	5	9	1.8
16	66	1	0.1	2	2	0.4
71	298	1	0.1	5	13	4
82	350	1	0.1	5	14	2.8
64	268	1	0.1	4	9	3.2
60	254	1	0.1	4	11	3.7
62	264	1	0.1	5	10	4
16	68	1	0.1	1	2	1.7
85	354	4	0.5	8	3	3.7
25	105	1	0.1	2	3	1.2
8	35	Trace	Trace	1	1	0.6
58	238	5	0.4	2	2	0.7
18	78	Trace	Trace	1	4	0.8
10	41	Trace	Trace	0	2	0.6
26	112	Trace	Trace	0	7	0.7
20	85	1	0.2	3	1	2
16	68	1	0.1	2	1	2
32	138	1	0.3	3	3	2.8
5	20	Trace	Trace	0	1	0.5
14	55	Trace	Trace	1	2	1.8
19	80	Trace	Trace	1	3	2.3
16	67	1	0.1	1	2	1.9
13	57	Trace	Trace	1	2	1.4
24	102	Trace	Trace	1	5	1.9
12	52	1	0.1	0	3	1.1
14	60	1	0.1	0	3	1.5
28	117	1	0.1	0	6	1.9

VEGETABLES	AVERAGE PORTION g	GI	GL
Carrots, young	60	M	L
Carrots, young, raw	60	M	L
Cassava, baked	100	M	M
Cauliflower	90	L	L
Cauliflower, raw	90	L	L
Celeriac	30	L	L
Celeriac, raw	30	L	L
Celery	30	L	L
Chard, Swiss	90	L	L
Chicory, raw	28	L	L
Chilli peppers, capsicum red	10	L	L
Chinese leaf	40	L	L
Corn, on the cob	200	M	M
Courgettes	90	L	L
Courgettes, fried	90	L	L
Cress	5	L	L
Cucumber	23	L	L
Curly kale	95	L	L
Endive	30	L	L
Fennel, Florence	40	L	L
Garlic, raw	3	L	L
Gourd, karela, canned	30	L	L
Jackfruit, canned	60	L	L
Kohlrabi	60	L	L
Kohlrabi, cooked	90	L	L
Leeks	75	L	L
Lentils, canned in tomato sauce	80	M	L
Lentils, green or brown, whole, dried	80	L	L
Lentils, red, split, dried, boiled	80	L	L
Lettuce, Cos	80	L	L
Lettuce, Iceberg	80	L	L
Lettuce, Webbs Wonder	80	L	L
Mange-tout peas, boiled	90	L	L
Mange-tout peas, raw	80	L	L

Unless otherwise stated, vegetables are described as they would normally be eaten.

ENERGY kcal	ENERGY kJ	FAT g	SATURATED FAT g	PROTEIN g	CARBO-HYDRATE g	FIBRE g
13	56	1	0.1	0	3	1.4
18	75	1	0.1	0	4	1.4
155	661	1	0.1	1	40	1.7
25	105	1	0.2	3	2	1.4
31	128	1	0.2	3	3	1.6
5	19	Trace	Trace	0	1	1
5	22	Trace	Trace	0	1	1.1
2	10	Trace	Trace	0	0	0.3
18	76	Trace	Trace	2	3	1.8
3	13	1	0.1	0	1	0.3
3	11	Trace	Trace	0	0	0.1
5	20	Trace	Trace	0	1	0.5
132	560	3	0.4	5	23	2.6
17	73	1	0.1	2	2	1.1
57	239	4	0.5	2	2	1.1
1	3	Trace	Trace	0	0	0.1
2	9	Trace	Trace	0	0	0.1
23	95	1	0.2	2	1	2.7
4	16	0	0	1	0	0.6
5	20	Trace	Trace	0	1	1
3	12	0	0	0	0	0.1
3	11	Trace	Trace	0	0	0.7
62	264	Trace	Trace	0	16	0.9
14	57	Trace	Trace	1	2	1.3
16	69	Trace	Trace	1	3	1.7
16	65	1	0.1	1	2	1.3
44	189	Trace	Trace	4	7	1.4
84	357	1	0.1	7	14	3
80	339	Trace	Trace	6	14	1.5
13	52	1	0.1	1	1	1
10	42	Trace	Trace	1	2	0.5
10	44	Trace	Trace	1	2	0.6
23	100	0	Trace	2.9	3	2
26	109	0	Trace	2.9	3.4	1.8

VEGETABLES	AVERAGE PORTION g	GI	GL
Marrow	65	L	L
Mixed vegetables, frozen	90	L	L
Mushrooms			
Shiitake, steamed	40	L	L
Straw, canned	40	L	L
White, fried	44	L	L
White, raw	40	L	L
Okra	30	L	L
Onions	150	L	L
Onions, fried	40	L	L
Parsnips, raw	65	H	M
Parsnips, roasted without oil	90	H	M
Peas, canned	70	M	L
Peas, fresh	70	M	L
Peas, frozen	70	M	L
Peas, mange-tout, stir-fried	90	L	L
Peas, marrowfat, canned	80	M	L
Peas, mushy, canned	80	M	L
Peas, petit pois, canned	70	M	L
Peas, petit pois, frozen	70	M	L
Peas, sugar-snap	90	L	L
Pease pudding, canned	80	M	L
Peppers, capsicum, green	160	L	L
Peppers, capsicum, red	160	L	L
Peppers, capsicum, yellow	160	L	L
Plantain	200	L	M
Plantain, ripe, fried	200	L	M
Potatoes and potato products			
Chips, crinkle cut, frozen, fried	165	H	H
Chips, fine cut, frozen, fried	165	H	H
Chips, fried	165	H	H
Chips, shop bought, fried	165	H	H
Chips, straight cut, frozen, fried	165	H	H
Chips, thick cut, frozen, fried	165	H	H

Unless otherwise stated, vegetables are described as they would normally be eaten.

ENERGY kcal	ENERGY kJ	FAT g	SATURATED FAT g	PROTEIN g	CARBO-HYDRATE g	FIBRE g
6	25	Trace	Trace	0	1	0.4
38	162	Trace	Trace	3	6	2.9
22	93	Trace	0	1	5	0.8
6	25	Trace	Trace	1	0	1
69	284	7	0.9	1	0	0.7
5	22	Trace	0	1	0	0.4
8	36	1	0.1	1	1	1.1
54	225	Trace	Trace	2	12	2.1
66	274	4	0.6	1	6	1.2
43	181	1	0.1	1	8	3.1
102	427	6	Trace	1	12	4.2
56	237	1	0.1	4	9	3.6
55	230	1	0.2	5	7	3.2
48	204	1	0.1	4	7	3.6
64	268	4	0.4	3	3	2.2
80	329	1	0.1	6	14	3.3
65	276	1	0.1	5	11	1.4
32	132	1	0.1	4	3	3
34	144	1	0.1	4	4	3.2
30	125	1	0.1	3	4	1.2
74	316	1	0.1	5	13	1.4
24	104	1	0.2	1	4	2.6
51	214	1	0.2	2	10	2.6
42	181	Trace	Trace	2	8	2.7
224	954	1	0.2	2	57	2.4
534	2252	1	2	3	95	4.6
479	2001	28	5.1	6	55	3.6
601	2515	35	6.6	7	68	4.5
312	1313	11	1.5	6	50	3.6
394	1652	20	2.6	5	50	3.6
450	1889	22	4.1	7	59	4
386	1622	17	3.1	6	56	4

VEGETABLES	AVERAGE PORTION g	GI	GL
Croquettes, fried	180	H	H
Duchesse	120	H	H
French fries	110	H	H
Microwave chips	165	H	H
Instant mash, made with semi-skimmed milk	60	H	M
Instant mash, made with water	60	H	M
Instant mash, made with whole milk	60	H	M
New, canned	165	M	M
New, chipped, fried	165	H	H
New, in skins, boiled	175	H	H
Old, baked	180	H	M
Old, boiled	175	H	M
Old, mashed with butter	120	H	M
Old, mashed with polyunsaturated fat spread	120	H	M
Old, roast	130	H	M
Oven chips, frozen	165	H	H
Oven chips, thick cut, frozen	165	H	H
Waffles, frozen	90	H	H
Wedges, baked	180	H	H
Pumpkin	60	H	L
Raddiccio, raw	30	L	L
Radishes, red, raw	48	L	L
Salad onions	10	L	L
Sauerkraut	30	L	L
Spinach	90	L	L
Spinach, cooked	90	L	L
Split peas, dried, boiled	90	L	L
Spring greens, boiled	95	L	L
Spring onions	10	L	L
Squash, acorn, baked	65	L	L
Squash, butternut, baked	65	L	L
Squash, spaghetti, baked	65	L	L

Unless otherwise stated, vegetables are described as they would normally be eaten.

ENERGY kcal	ENERGY kJ	FAT g	SATURATED FAT g	PROTEIN g	CARBO-HYDRATE g	FIBRE g
385	1607	24	3.1	7	39	2.3
148	622	6	3.6	4	20	1.4
308	1291	17	6.4	4	37	2.3
365	1535	17	3	6	53	4.8
42	178	1	0.2	1	9	0.6
34	147	Trace	Trace	1	8	0.6
46	193	1	0.4	1	9	0.6
104	447	Trace	Trace	2	25	1.3
376	1582	16	2	7	55	2.8
116	492	1	0.2	2	27	2.6
245	1046	Trace	Trace	7	57	4.9
126	536	Trace	Trace	3	30	2.1
125	526	5	3.4	2	19	1.3
125	526	5	1.1	2	19	1.3
194	819	6	0.8	4	34	2.3
267	1134	7	3	5	49	3.3
259	1096	7	2.8	5	46	3
180	758	12	1	2	28	2
245	1046	Trace	Trace	7	57	4.9
8	34	1	0.1	0	1	0.7
4	17	Trace	Trace	0	1	0.5
6	24	0	0	0	1	0.4
2	10	0	0	0	0	0.2
3	11	Trace	Trace	0	0	0.7
23	93	1	0.1	3	1	1.9
17	71	1	0.1	2	1	1.9
113	484	1	0.2	7	20	2.4
19	78	1	0.1	2	2	2.5
2	10	0	0	0	0	0.2
36	152	Trace	Trace	1	8	2.1
21	89	Trace	Trace	1	5	0.9
15	62	Trace	0.1	0	3	1.4

VEGETABLES

	AVERAGE PORTION g	GI	GL
Swede	60	H	L
Sweet potato, raw	130	L	M
Sweet potato, baked	130	M	H
Sweetcorn, baby, canned	60	M	M
Sweetcorn kernels, canned, reheated	85	M	M
Tomatoes	85	L	L
Tomatoes, canned, not drained	200	L	L
Tomatoes, cherry	90	L	L
Tomatoes, fried	85	L	L
Tomatoes, grilled	85	L	L
Turnips	60	L	L
Water chestnuts, canned	28	L	L
Watercress	20	L	L
Yam, raw	130	L	M
Yam, baked	130	M	M
Yam, steamed	130	M	M

PREPARED SALADS

Baby leaf salad	50	L	L
Bean salad	200	L	L
Beetroot salad	100	M	L
Carrot and nut salad with French dressing	95	L	L
Coleslaw, with mayonnaise	100	L	L
Coleslaw, with reduced-calorie dressing	100	L	L
Coleslaw, with vinaigrette	100	L	L
Florida salad	95	L	L
Greek salad	95	L	L
Green salad	95	L	L
Herb salad	50	L	L
Pasta salad	95	L	M
Pasta salad, wholemeal	95	L	M
Potato salad, with mayonnaise	85	H	H

Unless otherwise stated, vegetables are described as they would normally be eaten.

ENERGY kcal	ENERGY kJ	FAT g	SATURATED FAT g	PROTEIN g	CARBO-HYDRATE g	FIBRE g
7	28	Trace	Trace	0	1	0.4
109	465	1	0.1	1	27	3
150	634	1	0.3	2	36	4.3
14	58	Trace	Trace	2	1	0.9
104	441	1	0.2	2	23	1.2
14	62	1	0.1	1	3	0.9
32	138	Trace	Trace	2	6	1.4
16	68	1	0.1	1	3	0.9
77	320	7	0.9	1	4	1.1
42	179	1	0.3	2	8	2.5
7	31	1	Trace	0	1	1.1
9	37	Trace	Trace	0	3	2
4	19	1	0.1	1	0	0.3
173	738	1	0.1	2	43	1.8
199	846	1	0.1	3	49	2.2
148	634	1	0.1	2	37	1.7
9	40	Trace	Trace	Trace	2	0.7
294	1236	19	2	8	26	6
100	417	7	0.7	2	8	1.7
207	858	17	1.6	2	13	2.3
258	939	26	3.9	1	4	1.4
67	280	5	0.5	1	6	1.4
87	364	4	0.5	1	12	1.7
213	790	19	2.9	1	9	1
124	513	12	3.1	3	2	0.8
11	48	0	Trace	1	2	1
9	40	Trace	Trace	Trace	Trace	0.7
121	473	7	1	2	13	1.5
124	493	7	1	3	13	2.6
203	757	18	2.6	1	10	0.8

	AVERAGE PORTION g	GI	GL
PREPARED SALADS			
Potato salad, with reduced-calorie mayonnaise	85	H	H
Rice salad	90	H	H
Rice salad, brown	95	M	H
Rocket salad	25	L	L
Tabbouleh	100	M	H
Tomato and onion salad	90	L	L
Waldorf salad	90	L	L
VEGETABLE DISHES, HOMEMADE			
Bean loaf	90	L	L
Bhaji, aubergine, pea, potato and cauliflower	70	M	H
Bhaji, potato and cauliflower, fried	70	M	H
Bhaji, potato and onion	70	M	H
Broccoli in cheese sauce, made with semi-skimmed milk	190	L	M
Broccoli in cheese sauce, made with whole milk	190	L	L
Bubble and squeak, fried	140	M	H
Casserole, vegetable	220	M	H
Cauliflower cheese, made with semi-skimmed milk	200	L	M
Cauliflower cheese, made with whole milk	200	L	M
Cauliflower in white sauce, made with skimmed milk	200	L	M
Cauliflower in white sauce, made with whole milk	200	L	M
Chilli, bean and lentil	290	L	M
Chilli, vegetable	220	L	L
Curry, chickpea	210	L	L
Curry, potato and pea	290	M	H

Unless otherwise stated, vegetables are described as they would normally be eaten.

ENERGY kcal	ENERGY kJ	FAT g	SATURATED FAT g	PROTEIN g	CARBO-HYDRATE g	FIBRE g
82	349	3	0.3	1	13	0.7
149	628	7	1	3	21	0.6
159	668	7	1	3	23	1
3	12	Trace	Trace	Trace	Trace	0.2
119	496	5	0.4	3	17	1
65	272	5	0.6	1	4	0.9
174	662	16	2.1	1	7	1.2
134	564	7	0.7	6	14	3.9
49	209	2	0.2	2	7	2
214	888	15	1.8	5	14	2.7
112	468	7	4.6	1	12	1.1
211	880	14	7.2	12	9	2.9
224	939	16	8.2	12	9	2.9
174	727	13	1.4	2	14	2.1
114	486	1	0.2	5	23	4.6
200	840	13	6	12	10	2.6
210	880	14	6.6	12	10	2.6
122	512	6	2.2	7	10	2.2
136	568	8	3.2	7	10	2.2
264	1111	8	0.9	15	38	10.4
125	532	1	0.2	7	24	5.7
227	956	8	0.8	13	30	6.9
267	1122	11	1.2	8	38	7

VEGETABLE DISHES, HOMEMADE	AVERAGE PORTION g	GI	GL
Curry, vegetable	200	L	L
Dahl, mung bean, dried, boiled	60	L	L
Dahl, pigeon peas, dried, boiled	60	L	L
Falafel, fried	100	L	M
Lentil and nut roast	100	L	L
Lentil pie	100	M	M
Lentil roast	100	L	L
Lentil soup	220	L	L
Minestrone soup	220	L	L
Moussaka, vegetable	330	M	H
Pakora, potato and cauliflower, fried	70	M	M
Pasty, vegetable	155	M	M
Pasty, vegetable, wholemeal	155	M	M
Peppers, stuffed with rice	175	M	H
Peppers, stuffed with vegetables, cheese topping	175	M	M
Quiche, broccoli	140	M	M
Quiche, broccoli, wholemeal	140	M	M
Quiche, cauliflower cheese	140	M	M
Quiche, cauliflower cheese, wholemeal	140	M	M
Quiche, cheese and egg	140	M	M
Quiche, cheese and egg, wholemeal	140	M	M
Quiche, cheese and mushroom	140	M	M
Quiche, cheese and mushroom, wholemeal	140	M	M
Quiche, cheese, onion and potato	140	M	M
Quiche, cheese, onion and potato, wholemeal	140	M	M
Quiche, mushroom	140	M	M
Quiche, mushroom, wholemeal	140	M	M
Quiche, spinach	140	M	M
Quiche, spinach, wholemeal	140	M	M
Quiche, vegetable	140	M	M
Quiche, vegetable, wholemeal	140	M	M

Unless otherwise stated, vegetables are described as they would normally be eaten.

ENERGY kcal	ENERGY kJ	FAT g	SATURATED FAT g	PROTEIN g	CARBO-HYDRATE g	FIBRE g
176	736	12	1.2	5	14	5
55	235	1	0.1	5	9	1.8
71	298	1	0.1	5	13	4
179	750	11	1.1	6	16	3.4
222	929	12	1.8	11	19	3.8
156	659	4	0.5	7	24	3.8
139	588	3	0.4	8	22	3.4
218	920	8	2.9	9.7	27.9	2.4
139	581	7	1.4	4	16.7	2
452	1888	31	9.2	15	30	4
214	888	15	1.8	5	14	2.7
425	1783	23	5.7	6	52	2.9
406	1702	24	5.7	8	43	6.4
149	630	4	0.7	3	27	2.3
194	810	12	3.5	6	17	2.6
349	1455	21	8.3	12	30	1.7
337	1408	21	8.3	13	25	3.8
277	1156	18	7.1	7	24	1.5
269	1121	18	7.1	8	20	3.1
440	1834	31	14.4	18	24	0.8
431	1796	31	14.6	18	20	2.7
396	1655	26	10.8	15	26	1.3
388	1616	27	10.8	16	22	3.1
480	2005	33	16	18	28	1.4
472	1966	34	16.1	19	25	3.1
398	1659	27	12.2	14	26	1.3
388	1618	28	12.2	15	21	3.1
287	1203	18	5.6	14	18	2
281	1176	18	5.6	15	16	3.2
295	1238	18	6	7	28	2.1
286	1197	18	6	8	24	3.9

VEGETABLE DISHES, HOMEMADE	AVERAGE PORTION g	GI	GL
Refried beans	90	L	L
Rice and blackeye beans	200	M	M
Rice and blackeye beans, brown rice	200	M	M
Rissoles, chickpea, fried	100	L	L
Rissoles, lentil, fried	100	L	L
Tomato soup, cream of	220	L	L
Vegetable bake	260	L	L
Vine leaves, stuffed with rice	80	L	M

VEGETARIAN PRODUCTS AND DISHES

	AVERAGE PORTION g	GI	GL
Beanburger, aduki, fried	90	M	L
Beanburger, butter bean, fried	90	M	L
Beanburger, red kidney bean, fried	90	M	L
Beanburger, soya, fried	90	M	L
Quorn™, myco-protein	90	L	L
Soya mince	28	L	L
Tempeh	60	L	L
Tofu, fried	80	L	L
Tofu, steamed	80	L	L
Tofu, steamed, fried	80	L	L
Tofu burger, baked	9	L	L
Vegebanger mix, made with water and egg, fried	56	L	L
Vegebanger mix, made with water, fried	56	L	L
Vegeburger, fried	56	L	L
Vegeburger, grilled	56	L	L
Vegeburger mix, made with water and egg, fried	56	M	L
Vegeburger mix, made with water and egg, grilled	56	M	L
Vegeburger mix, made with water, fried	56	M	L
Vegeburger mix, made with water, grilled	56	M	L

Unless otherwise stated, vegetables are described as they would normally be eaten.

ENERGY kcal	ENERGY kJ	FAT g	SATURATED FAT g	PROTEIN g	CARBO-HYDRATE g	FIBRE g
211	885	12	2.7	9	18	6.3
366	1556	7	3	12	68	2.8
350	1488	7	3	11	66	3.6
243	1016	17	1.9	8	16	4.1
211	886	11	1.3	9	22	3.6
114	482	7	1.1	1.8	13	1.5
330	1383	18	7.8	11	32	2.9
210	875	14	2.1	2	19	1.0
165	695	6	0.9	7	21	3.9
172	722	10	1.1	5	17	3.7
183	768	10	1.1	6	20	4.4
174	725	10	1.4	10	12	4.2
77	326	3	Trace	11	2	4.3
99	413	0.3	0	15	9	6
100	418	4	2	12	4	2.6
242	1011	20	2.3	17	3	1
58	243	3	0.4	6	1	1
209	869	14	2.3	19	2	1
11	45	0	0.1	1	1	0.2
157	659	10	2.5	10	7	1.9
137	572	9	2	8	7	1.8
137	571	10	1.7	9	4	2
110	460	6	1.7	9	4	2.4
122	511	7	1.6	8	7	1.8
91	385	4	1.2	8	7	1.8
115	482	6	1.3	7	8	2
84	356	3	1	7	8	2

BEEF

	AVERAGE PORTION g	GI	GL
Braising steak, braised	140	M	L
Braising steak, untrimmed, braised	140	M	L
Braising steak, slow cooked	140	M	L
Braising steak, untrimmed, slow cooked	140	M	L
Fillet steak, fried	172	M	L
Fillet steak, untrimmed, fried	172	M	L
Fillet steak, grilled	168	M	L
Fillet steak, untrimmed, grilled	168	M	L
Flank, pot roasted	140	M	L
Flank, untrimmed, pot roasted	140	M	L
Fore rib, roasted	90	M	L
Fore rib, untrimmed, roasted	90	M	L
Mince, extra lean, stewed	140	M	L
Mince, microwaved	140	M	L
Mince, stewed	140	M	L
Rib roast, roasted	90	M	L
Rib roast, untrimmed, roasted	90	M	L
Rump steak, grilled	163	M	L
Rump steak, untrimmed, grilled	163	M	L
Rump steak, fried	166	M	L
Rump steak, untrimmed, fried	166	M	L
Rump steak strips, stir-fried	103	M	L
Rump steak strips, untrimmed, stir-fried	103	M	L
Silverside, pot roasted	140	M	L
Silverside, untrimmed, pot roasted	140	M	L
Silverside, salted, boiled	140	M	L
Silverside, untrimmed, salted, boiled	140	M	L
Sirloin joint, roasted	90	M	L
Sirloin joint, untrimmed, roasted	90	M	L
Sirloin steak, fried	169	M	L
Sirloin steak, untrimmed, fried	169	M	L
Sirloin steak, grilled medium rare	166	M	L
Sirloin steak, untrimmed, grilled medium rare	166	M	L

Unless otherwise stated, all meat is lean and trimmed, and all chops and cutlets are boned. Steaks are medium-sized. Unless stated otherwise, all dishes are homemade.

ENERGY kcal	ENERGY kJ	FAT g	SATURATED FAT g	PROTEIN g	CARBO-HYDRATE g	FIBRE g
315	1322	14	5.7	48	0	0
344	1441	18	7.4	46	0	0
276	1156	11	4.8	44	0	0
304	1270	16	6.7	41	0	0
316	1328	14	5.8	49	0	0
330	1384	15	6.7	49	0	0
316	1329	13	6	49	0	0
336	1410	16	7.4	48	0	0
354	1483	20	8	45	0	0
433	1800	31	12.7	38	0	0
212	889	10	4.6	30	0	0
270	1125	18	8.3	26	0	0
248	1039	12	5.3	35	0	0
368	1534	25	10.6	37	0	0
293	1218	19	8.3	31	0	0
212	889	10	4.6	30	0	0
270	1125	18	8.3	26	0	0
287	1208	9	3.9	51	0	0
331	1384	15	6.5	48	0	0
304	1278	11	4.2	51	0	0
378	1582	21	8.1	47	0	0
214	901	9	3.4	33	0	0
255	1069	15	5.8	31	0	0
270	1135	9	3.5	48	0	0
346	1448	19	7.8	43	0	0
258	1081	10	3.5	43	0	0
314	1312	18	6.6	39	0	0
169	712	6	2.6	29	0	0
210	876	11	5	27	0	0
319	1340	14	5.7	49	0	0
394	1646	24	10.1	45	0	0
292	1223	13	5.6	44	0	0
354	1474	21	9.3	41	0	0

BEEF

	AVERAGE PORTION g	GI	GL
Sirloin steak, grilled rare	166	M	L
Sirloin steak, untrimmed, grilled rare	166	M	L
Sirloin steak, grilled well done	166	M	L
Sirloin steak, untrimmed, grilled well done	166	M	L
Stewing steak, stewed	140	M	L
Stewing steak, untrimmed, stewed	140	M	L
Topside, roasted medium rare	90	M	L
Topside, untrimmed, roasted medium rare	90	M	L
Topside, roasted well done	90	M	L
Topside, untrimmed, roasted well done	90	M	L

LAMB

Best end neck cutlets, grilled	50	M	L
Best end neck cutlets, untrimmed, grilled	50	M	L
Breast, roasted	90	M	L
Breast, untrimmed, roasted	90	M	L
Chump chops, fried	70	M	L
Chump chops, untrimmed, fried	70	M	L
Chump steaks, untrimmed, fried	90	M	L
Kebabs, grilled	90	M	L
Leg, roasted medium	90	M	L
Leg, untrimmed, roasted medium	90	M	L
Leg, roasted well done	90	M	L
Leg, untrimmed, roasted well done	90	M	L
Leg chops, untrimmed, grilled	70	M	L
Leg half fillet, braised	70	M	L
Leg half fillet, untrimmed, braised	70	M	L
Leg half knuckle, pot roasted	90	M	L
Leg half knuckle, untrimmed, pot roasted	90	M	L
Leg joint, roasted	90	M	L

Unless otherwise stated, all meat is lean and trimmed, and all chops and cutlets are boned. Steaks are medium-sized. Unless stated otherwise, all dishes are homemade.

ENERGY kcal	ENERGY kJ	FAT g	SATURATED FAT g	PROTEIN g	CARBO-HYDRATE g	FIBRE g
276	1157	11	5	44	0	0
359	1494	21	9.6	42	0	0
374	1565	16	7.3	56	0	0
427	1781	24	10.8	53	0	0
259	1088	9	3.2	45	0	0
284	1193	13	5.2	41	0	0
158	662	5	1.9	29	0	0
200	837	10	4.3	27	0	0
182	764	6	2.3	33	0	0
220	918	11	4.7	30	0	0
118	493	7	3.3	14	0	0
171	710	14	6.6	12	0	0
246	1024	17	7.7	24	0	0
323	1338	27	12.9	20	0	0
149	624	8	3.5	20	0	0
216	895	16	7.6	17	0	0
255	1058	18	8.5	22	0	0
259	1079	17	8.1	26	0	0
183	768	8	3.4	27	0	0
216	904	13	5.3	25	0	0
187	786	8	3.3	28	0	0
218	909	12	5.1	27	0	0
155	648	8	3.5	20	0	0
143	597	7	3.2	19	0	0
179	748	12	5.4	18	0	0
181	760	8	3.5	26	0	0
213	889	12	5.4	25	0	0
189	791	9	3.1	28	0	0

LAMB	AVERAGE PORTION g	GI	GL
Leg joint, untrimmed, roasted	90	M	L
Leg steaks, grilled	90	M	L
Leg steaks, untrimmed, grilled	90	M	L
Loin chops, grilled	70	M	L
Loin chops, untrimmed, grilled	70	M	L
Loin chops, roasted	70	M	L
Loin chops, untrimmed, roasted	70	M	L
Loin joint, roasted	90	M	L
Loin joint, untrimmed, roasted	90	M	L
Mince, stewed	90	M	L
Neck fillet, grilled	90	M	L
Neck fillet, untrimmed, grilled	90	M	L
Neck fillet strips, stir-fried	90	M	L
Neck fillet strips, untrimmed, stir-fried	90	M	L
Rack of lamb, roasted	90	M	L
Rack of lamb, untrimmed, roasted	90	M	L
Shoulder half bladeside, pot roasted	90	M	L
Shoulder half bladeside, untrimmed, pot roasted	90	M	L
Shoulder half knuckle, braised	90	M	L
Shoulder half knuckle, untrimmed, braised	90	M	L
Shoulder joint, roasted	90	M	L
Shoulder joint, untrimmed, roasted	90	M	L
Shoulder, roasted	90	M	L
Shoulder, untrimmed, roasted	90	M	L
Stewing lamb, stewed	260	M	L
Stewing lamb, untrimmed, stewed	260	M	L

Unless otherwise stated, all meat is lean and trimmed, and all chops and
cutlets are boned. Steaks are medium-sized. Unless stated otherwise, all
dishes are homemade.

ENERGY kcal	ENERGY kJ	FAT g	SATURATED FAT g	PROTEIN g	CARBO- HYDRATE g	FIBRE g
212	887	12	4.2	27	0	0
178	746	8	3.2	26	0	0
208	868	12	5	25	0	0
149	624	7	3.4	20	0	0
214	888	15	7.4	19	0	0
180	754	9	4.3	24	0	0
251	1043	19	9	20	0	0
188	788	10	4.4	25	0	0
273	1133	20	9.5	23	0	0
187	783	11	5.2	22	0	0
256	1063	17	7.8	25	0	0
272	1131	20	9.3	24	0	0
250	1040	18	7.4	22	0	0
271	1124	21	8.9	21	0	0
203	848	12	5.6	24	0	0
327	1355	27	13.3	21	0	0
211	878	13	5.8	24	0	0
292	1212	23	10.8	21	0	0
191	797	11	4.9	23	0	0
272	1130	21	9.7	21	0	0
212	884	12	5.6	26	0	0
254	1056	18	8.4	23	0	0
196	819	11	5	24	0	0
268	1114	20	9.4	22	0	0
624	2600	38	16.9	69	0	0
725	3013	52	23.9	63	0	0

MEAT DISHES	AVERAGE PORTION g	GI	GL
Beef bourguignon	260	M	L
Beef casserole, canned	270	M	L
Beef casserole, made with canned cook-in sauce	300	M	L
Beef hotpot with potatoes, shop bought	260	M	L
Beef stew	280	M	L
Beef stew, made with lean beef	260	M	L
Beef stew and dumplings	260	M	L
Cannelloni, shop bought	260	M	L
Chilli con carne	220	M	L
Chilli con carne, shop bought	220	M	L
Corned beef hash	300	M	L
Cottage pie	310	M	L
Cottage pie, shop bought	310	M	L
Irish stew	330	M	L
Irish stew, made with lean beef	330	M	L
Lamb hotpot with potatoes, shop bought	260	M	L
Lancashire hotpot	260	M	L
Lasagne, shop bought	420	M	L
Meatloaf	100	M	L
Moussaka	330	M	L
Moussaka, shop bought	330	M	L
Pork and beef meatballs in tomato sauce	160	M	L
Pork casserole, made with canned cook-in sauce	260	M	L
Sausage casserole	350	M	L
Shepherd's pie	310	M	L
Shepherd's pie, shop bought	310	M	L
Toad in the hole	160	M	L
Toad in the hole, made with skimmed milk and reduced-fat sausages	160	M	L

Unless otherwise stated, all meat is lean and trimmed, and all chops and cutlets are boned. Steaks are medium-sized. Unless stated otherwise, all dishes are homemade.

ENERGY kcal	ENERGY kJ	FAT g	SATURATED FAT g	PROTEIN g	CARBO-HYDRATE g	FIBRE g
328	1368	17	5.5	36	7	1
211	886	7	3.8	19	19	2.7
408	1707	20	8.1	45	14	2.7
281	1183	11	4.4	19	28	2.3
316	1328	14	4.2	34	14	2
263	1102	9	2.3	32	13	1.8
499	2090	27	12.5	26	41	2.6
315	1326	13	5.2	17	35	3.1
286	1199	17	6.6	20	10	2.4
211	889	9	4.2	17	16	3.1
423	1776	18	9.9	31	37	3
391	1634	21	7.8	20	32	2.8
344	1448	17	7.4	14	37	2.8
399	1676	21	9.6	25	29	3.3
366	1541	17	7.3	26	29	3.3
281	1183	11	4.4	19	28	2.3
289	1206	14	5.5	23	20	2.3
601	2533	26	11.8	31	66	2.9
214	894	11	4.1	17	13	0.5
403	1680	26	11.9	28	15	3.3
462	1934	27	9.6	27	28	2.6
202	840	12	4.4	16	8	1.2
398	1664	20	6.8	44	10	0
578	2405	38	12.3	42	18	3.1
391	1634	21	7.8	20	32	2.8
344	1448	17	7.4	14	37	2.8
443	1853	28	10.7	19	31	1.8
320	1344	14	4.6	20	31	1.9

MEAT PRODUCTS

	AVERAGE PORTION g	GI	GL
Black pudding, dry-fried	75	M	L
Corned beef	50	M	L
Faggots in gravy, shop bought	150	M	L
Haggis, boiled	85	M	L
Luncheon meat, canned	40	M	L
Meatloaf, shop bought	100	M	L
Scotch eggs, shop bought	120	M	L
White pudding	75	M	L

SAUSAGES

Beef sausages, fried	40	M	L
Beef sausages, grilled	40	M	L
Bratwurst	75	M	L
Chorizo	30	M	L
Frankfurter	47	M	L
Garlic sausage	40	M	L
Kabana	30	M	L
Mortadella	24	M	L
Pastrami	50	M	L
Pork and beef sausages, grilled	40	M	L
Pork and beef, economy sausages, fried	40	M	L
Pork and beef, economy sausages, grilled	40	M	L
Pork sausages, fried	40	M	L
Pork sausages, grilled	40	M	L
Pork sausages, frozen, fried	40	M	L
Pork sausages, frozen, grilled	40	M	L
Pork sausages, reduced-fat, fried	40	M	L
Pork sausages, reduced-fat, grilled	40	M	L
Premium sausages, fried	40	M	L
Premium sausages, grilled	40	M	L
Salami	12	M	L
Saveloy, unbattered, shop bought	65	M	L

Unless otherwise stated, all meat is lean and trimmed, and all chops and
cutlets are boned. Steaks are medium-sized. Unless stated otherwise, all
dishes are homemade.

ENERGY kcal	ENERGY kJ	FAT g	SATURATED FAT g	PROTEIN g	CARBO-HYDRATE g	FIBRE g
223	927	16	6.4	8	12	0.2
103	430	5	2.8	13	1	0
222	929	11	3.8	12	19	0.3
264	1098	18	6.5	9	16	0.2
112	463	10	3.5	5	1	0.1
216	900	16	5.6	17	1	0.5
301	1255	5.2	19	14	16	0
338	1407	24	8	5	27	1
112	464	8	3	5	5	0.3
111	463	8	3.2	5	5	0.3
195	811	16	6	12	2	Trace
87	362	7	2.9	5	1	Trace
135	559	12	4.3	6	1	0
99	412	8	2.9	6	0	Trace
92	383	8	3.4	5	0	Trace
79	328	7	2.8	3	0	Trace
62	259	2	0.9	10	1	0
108	448	8	3	5	4	0.5
99	414	7	1.8	5	5	0.5
103	429	7	1.9	5	5	0.5
123	512	10	3.4	6	4	0.3
118	488	9	3.2	6	4	0.3
126	525	10	3.5	6	4	0.3
116	482	8	3	6	4	0.3
84	352	5	1.7	6	4	0.6
92	384	6	2	6	4	0.6
110	457	8	3.1	6	3	0.3
117	486	9	3.3	7	3	0.3
53	218	5	1.8	3	0	0
192	801	18	3.6	9	7	0.5

	AVERAGE PORTION g	GI	GL
BEEFBURGERS			
Beefburgers, fried	36	M	L
Beefburgers, grilled	100	M	L
Beefburgers, fried	100	M	L
Beefburgers, grilled	100	M	L
Beefburgers, low-fat, fried	100	M	L
Beefburgers, low-fat, grilled	100	M	L
Beefburgers in gravy, canned	100	M	L
PIES AND PASTIES			
Beef pie, shop bought	141	M	L
Cornish pasty	155	M	L
Cornish pasty, shop bought	155	M	L
Lamb samosa, baked	70	M	L
Lamb samosa, deep-fried	70	M	L
Pork and egg pie	60	M	L
Pork pie	60	M	L
Pork pie, mini	50	M	L
Sausage rolls, flaky pastry	60	M	L
Sausage rolls, shortcrust pastry	60	M	L
Steak and kidney pie, double crust	120	M	L
Steak and kidney pie, shop bought	141	M	L
OFFAL			
Heart, lamb, roasted	200	M	L
Heart, lamb, stewed	200	M	L
Heart, ox, stewed	200	M	L
Heart, pig, stewed	100	M	L
Kidney, lamb, fried	35	M	L
Kidney, ox, stewed	112	M	L
Kidney, pig, fried	140	M	L
Kidney, pig, stewed	140	M	L
Liver, calf, fried	100	M	L

Unless otherwise stated, all meat is lean and trimmed, and all chops and cutlets are boned. Steaks are medium-sized. Unless stated otherwise, all dishes are homemade.

ENERGY kcal	ENERGY kJ	FAT g	SATURATED FAT g	PROTEIN g	CARBO-HYDRATE g	FIBRE g
118	493	9	3.9	10	0	0
326	1355	24	10.9	27	0	0
303	1261	23	8.7	24	1	0.2
287	1194	20	8.8	25	1	0.2
193	807	11	5	24	0	0
178	745	10	4.4	23	1	0
171	713	12	4.8	12	5	Trace
437	1826	24	11.8	12	38	0.7
456	1905	28	9.8	10	43	2.6
414	1731	25	9.1	10	39	1.4
187	781	10	2.5	8	16	1.2
265	1097	22	3.3	6	12	0.8
178	740	13	4.4	6	10	0.5
228	947	18	6.8	6	11	0.5
196	815	14	5.7	5	13	0.5
238	991	17	6.5	6	15	0.8
229	953	16	5.8	6	17	0.9
406	1694	26	9.7	16	27	1.1
437	1826	24	11.8	12	38	0.7
452	1888	28	6.2	51	0	0
312	1308	15	6	24	20	0
314	1322	10	5	56	0	0
162	678	7	1.3	25	0	0
66	274	4	0.4	8	0	0
155	648	5	1.6	27	0	0
283	1187	13	2.1	41	0	0
214	897	9	2.8	34	0	0
176	734	10	2.7	22	Trace	0

OFFAL	AVERAGE PORTION g	GI	GL
Liver, chicken, fried	70	M	L
Liver, lamb, fried	100	M	L
Liver, ox, stewed	70	M	L
Liver, pig, stewed	70	M	L
Liver and bacon, fried	100	M	L
Liver and onions, stewed	142	M	L
Liver sausage	40	M	L
Oxtail, stewed	260	M	L
Sweetbread, lamb, fried	100	M	L
Tongue	50	M	L
Tongue, canned	50	M	L
Tongue, ox, stewed	50	M	L
Tongue, sheep, stewed	50	M	L
Tripe and onions, stewed	100	M	L

PORK, BACON AND HAM			
Bacon			
Collar joint, boiled	46	M	L
Collar joint, untrimmed, boiled	46	M	L
Loin steaks, grilled	100	M	L
Rashers, back, dry-cured, grilled	100	M	L
Rashers, back, dry-fried	100	M	L
Rashers, back, grilled	100	M	L
Rashers, back, untrimmed, grilled	100	M	L
Rashers, back, grilled crispy	100	M	L
Rashers, back, reduced salt, grilled	100	M	L
Rashers, back, smoked, grilled	100	M	L
Rashers, back, sweetcure, grilled	100	M	L
Rashers, back, 'tendersweet', grilled	100	M	L
Rashers, middle, fried	100	M	L
Rashers, middle, grilled	100	M	L
Rashers, streaky, fried	100	M	L
Rashers, streaky, grilled	100	M	L

Unless otherwise stated, all meat is lean and trimmed, and all chops and cutlets are boned. Steaks are medium-sized. Unless stated otherwise, all dishes are homemade.

ENERGY kcal	ENERGY kJ	FAT g	SATURATED FAT g	PROTEIN g	CARBO-HYDRATE g	FIBRE g
118	494	6	3.5	15	Trace	0
237	989	13	4.9	30	Trace	0
139	582	7	2.5	17	2	0
132	555	6	1.8	18	2	0
247	1030	15	2.1	29	Trace	0
210	879	11	2.1	21	8	1.4
90	377	7	2.1	5	2	0.3
632	2636	35	12	79	0	0
217	910	11	5	29	0	0
101	418	7	3	9	Trace	Trace
107	442	8	3.2	8	Trace	0
121	504	9	3	10	0	0
145	599	12	5	9	0	0
93	393	3	1.5	8	10	0.7
88	368	4	1.7	12	0	0
150	619	12	4.9	9	0	0
191	799	10	3.5	26	0	0
257	1071	16	6	28	0	0
295	1225	22	8.3	24	0	0
214	892	12	4.6	26	0	0
287	1194	22	8.1	23	0	0
313	1308	19	7.1	36	0	0
282	1172	21	7.8	24	0	0
293	1216	22	8.3	23	0	0
258	1074	17	6.6	24	2	0
213	889	12	4.5	26	Trace	0
350	1452	29	9.8	23	0	0
307	1276	23	8.4	25	0	0
335	1389	27	9.1	24	0	0
337	1400	27	9.8	24	0	0

PORK, BACON AND HAM

	AVERAGE PORTION g	GI	GL
Belly joint, untrimmed, roasted	110	M	L
Belly, untrimmed, grilled	110	M	L
Chump chops, untrimmed, fried	170	M	L
Chump steaks, untrimmed, fried	170	M	L
Crackling, cooked	50	M	L
Fillet, grilled, lean	120	M	L
Fillet, untrimmed, grilled	120	M	L
Fillet strips, stir-fried, lean	90	M	L
Gammon			
Joint, boiled	170	M	L
Rashers, grilled	100	M	L
Ham			
Ham, canned	90	M	L
Ham, Parma	47	M	L
Ham, premium	56	M	L
Pork shoulder, cured	100	M	L
Kebabs, grilled	90	M	L
Kebabs, untrimmed, grilled	90	M	L
Leg joint, untrimmed, frozen, roasted	90	M	L
Leg joint, roasted medium	90	M	L
Leg joint, untrimmed, roasted medium	90	M	L
Leg joint, roasted well done	90	M	L
Leg joint, untrimmed, roasted well done	90	M	L
Loin chops, grilled	75	M	L
Loin chops, untrimmed, grilled	75	M	L
Loin chops, grilled	120	M	L
Loin chops, untrimmed, grilled	120	M	L
Loin chops, roasted	75	M	L
Loin chops, untrimmed, roasted	75	M	L
Loin joint, pot roasted	90	M	L
Loin joint, untrimmed, pot roasted	90	M	L
Loin joint, roasted	90	M	L
Loin joint, untrimmed, roasted	90	M	L
Loin steaks, fried	120	M	L

Unless otherwise stated, all meat is lean and trimmed, and all chops and cutlets are boned. Steaks are medium-sized. Unless stated otherwise, all dishes are homemade.

ENERGY kcal	ENERGY kJ	FAT g	SATURATED FAT g	PROTEIN g	CARBO- HYDRATE g	FIBRE g
322	1341	24	8.1	28	0	0
352	1465	26	9	30	0	0
498	2069	37	11.9	42	0	0
369	1542	20	6.3	47	0	0
275	1140	23	7.7	18	0	0
204	863	5	1.8	40	0	0
214	899	6	2.3	40	0	0
164	688	5	1.2	29	0	0
347	1447	21	7	40	0	0
199	834	10	3.4	28	0	0
96	404	4	1.4	15	0	0
105	438	6	2	13	Trace	Trace
74	310	3	1	12	0	0
103	435	4	1.2	17	1	0
161	679	4	1.4	31	0	0
170	717	5	2	30	0	0
202	842	10	3.6	28	0	0
164	689	5	1.7	30	0	0
194	813	9	3.2	28	0	0
167	701	5	1.6	31	0	0
233	974	14	4.9	27	0	0
140	585	5	1.8	23	0	0
191	800	12	4.3	21	0	0
221	929	8	2.6	38	0	0
308	1289	19	6.7	35	0	0
181	758	8	2.8	28	0	0
226	942	14	5.3	24	0	0
177	744	7	2.6	28	0	0
275	1142	21	7.4	22	0	0
164	687	6	2.2	27	0	0
228	949	15	5.3	24	0	0
229	962	9	2.8	38	0	0

PORK, BACON AND HAM	AVERAGE PORTION g	GI	GL
Loin steaks, untrimmed, fried	120	M	L
Mince, stewed	90	M	L
Pork, diced, casseroled	90	M	L
Pork, diced, untrimmed, casseroled	90	M	L
Pork steaks, grilled	135	M	L
Pork steaks, untrimmed, grilled	135	M	L
Pork steaks, stewed	135	M	L
Pork steaks, untrimmed, stewed	135	M	L
Spare rib, untrimmed, grilled	110	M	L
Spare rib chops, braised	140	M	L
Spare rib chops, untrimmed, braised	140	M	L
Spare rib joint, pot roasted	90	M	L
Spare rib joint, untrimmed, pot roasted	90	M	L

Unless otherwise stated, all meat is lean and trimmed, and all chops and cutlets are boned. Steaks are medium-sized. Unless stated otherwise, all dishes are homemade.

ENERGY kcal	ENERGY kJ	FAT g	SATURATED FAT g	PROTEIN g	CARBO-HYDRATE g	FIBRE g
331	1378	22	7.2	33	0	0
172	720	9	3.5	22	0	0
166	698	6	1.7	29	0	0
166	698	6	1.8	28	0	0
228	963	5	1.8	46	0	0
267	1123	10	3.6	44	0	0
238	1000	6	1.8	45	0	0
269	1126	11	3.2	42	0	0
321	1340	21	8.3	32	0	0
298	1249	14	5	43	0	0
346	1446	21	7.7	39	0	0
181	759	8	2.9	27	0	0
234	973	16	6	22	0	0

CHICKEN

	AVERAGE PORTION g	GI	GL
Breast, casseroled	130	L	L
Breast, skinned, casseroled	130	L	L
Breast, grilled	130	L	L
Breast, grilled and skinned	130	L	L
Breast, skinned, grilled	130	L	L
Breast strips, stir-fried	90	L	L
Corn-fed chicken, roasted, dark meat	90	L	L
Corn-fed chicken, roasted, light meat	90	L	L
Dark meat, roasted	100	L	L
Drumsticks, casseroled	47	L	L
Drumsticks, skinned, casseroled	47	L	L
Drumsticks, roasted	47	L	L
Drumsticks, skinned, roasted	47	L	L
Leg quarter, casseroled	146	L	L
Leg quarter, skinned, casseroled	146	L	L
Leg quarter, roasted	146	L	L
Light meat, roasted	100	L	L
Thighs, casseroled	45	L	L
Thighs, skinned, boned and diced, casseroled	45	L	L
Wing quarter, casseroled	150	L	L
Wing quarter, skinned, casseroled	150	L	L
Wing quarter, roasted	150	L	L
Wings, grilled	100	L	L

CHICKEN PRODUCTS

Chicken fingers, baked	90	H	H
Chicken goujons, baked	90	H	H
Chicken in crumbs, stuffed with cheese and vegetables, baked	100	H	H
Chicken nugget	84	L	L
Chicken in white sauce, canned	100	L	L
Chicken Kiev, frozen, baked	170	H	H

Unless otherwise stated, chicken and turkey are neither skinned nor boned, game is skinned and trimmed and dishes are homemade.

ENERGY kcal	ENERGY kJ	FAT g	SATURATED FAT g	PROTEIN g	CARBO-HYDRATE g	FIBRE g
239	1004	11	3.1	35	0	0
148	628	7	2	37	0	0
225	946	8	1.2	38	0	0
191	807	4	1.2	39	0	0
192	814	4	0.8	42	0	0
145	609	4	0.8	27	0	0
167	695	9	2.5	22	0	0
127	536	4	1.1	23	0	0
196	819	11	2.9	24	0	0
102	425	7	1.8	10	0	0
87	363	5	1.2	11	0	0
87	364	4	1.2	12	0	0
71	301	2	0.7	13	0	0
317	1320	20	5.5	33	0	0
257	1075	12	3.4	37	0	0
345	1432	25	6.7	31	0	0
153	645	4	1	30	0	0
105	436	7	2	10	0	0
81	340	4	1.1	12	0	0
315	1316	19	5.3	37	0	0
246	1035	9	2.6	40	0	0
339	1415	21	5.9	37	0	0
274	1146	17	4.6	27	Trace	0
185	774	9	2.7	11	17	Trace
249	1045	13	3.6	17	18	0.6
230	963	14	4.1	16	11	0.9
276	1157	20	3.9	14.1	11.2	0
141	590	8	2.3	14	3	Trace
456	1902	29	12.1	32	19	1

	AVERAGE PORTION g	GI	GL
CHICKEN PRODUCTS			
Chicken pancakes, frozen, shallow-fried	100	M	M
Chicken roll	24	L	L
Chicken slices	80	L	L
CHICKEN PIES			
Chicken and mushroom pie, single crust	100	H	H
Chicken pie, individual, baked	130	H	H
CHICKEN DISHES			
Chicken chasseur	260	L	L
Chicken in sauce with vegetables	290	L	L
Chicken curry	350	L	L
Chicken curry, with bone	350	L	L
Chicken curry, without bone	300	L	L
Chicken fricassée	200	L	L
Chicken in white sauce, made with semi-skimmed milk	200		
Chicken in white sauce, made with whole milk	200	L	L
Chicken risotto	350	M	H
Coronation chicken	200	L	L
Lemon chicken	100	L	L
Tandoori chicken	100	L	L

Unless otherwise stated, chicken and turkey are neither skinned nor boned, game is skinned and trimmed and dishes are homemade.

ENERGY kcal	ENERGY kJ	FAT g	SATURATED FAT g	PROTEIN g	CARBO-HYDRATE g	FIBRE g	
260	1090	14	1.4	6	29	0.1	
31	132	1	0.4	4	1	Trace	
91	386	1	0.3	19	2	0	
200	836	10	4.5	13	14	0.6	
374	1563	21	9.1	12	32	1	
203	861	5	0.8	33	7	0.8	
336	1412	15	7	39	13	0.9	
522	2174	31	14	42	19	4.5	
539	2237	44	6	27	8	2.4	
615	2550	51	6.6	31	9	2.7	
214	896	12	4.8	22	6	1	
310	1298	16	5	34	10	0.2	
328	1376	18	6.2	34	10	0.2	
546	2310	10	4.5	31	84	Trace	
728	3012	63	10.4	33	6	Trace	
155	652	6	0.8	16	9	Trace	
214	897	11	3.3	27	2	Trace	

	AVERAGE PORTION g	GI	GL
GAME			
Duck meat and skin	185	L	L
Duck, roasted	185	L	L
Duck, untrimmed, roasted	185	L	L
Goose, roasted	185	L	L
Goose, untrimmed, roasted	185	L	L
Grouse, roasted	160	L	L
Pheasant, roasted	160	L	L
Pigeon, roasted	115	L	L
Rabbit, stewed	160	L	L
Venison, roasted	120	L	L
TURKEY			
Breast, grilled and skinned	90	L	L
Dark meat, roasted	90	L	L
Drumsticks, roasted	90	L	L
Drumsticks, roasted and skinned	90	L	L
Light meat, from self-basting bird, roasted	90	L	L
Light meat, roasted	90	L	L
Mince, stewed	90	L	L
Strips, stir-fried	90	L	L
Thighs, diced, skinned, boned, casseroled	90	L	L

Unless otherwise stated, chicken and turkey are neither skinned nor
boned, game is skinned and trimmed and dishes are homemade.

ENERGY kcal	ENERGY kJ	FAT g	SATURATED FAT g	PROTEIN g	CARBO-HYDRATE g	FIBRE g
783	3238	70	21.1	37	0	0
361	1508	19	6.1	47	0	0
783	3238	92	21.1	37	0	0
590	2455	41	13.7	54	0	0
557	2316	39	12.2	51	0	0
205	869	3	0.8	44	0	0
352	1469	5	0.6	45	0	0
215	903	9	3	33	0	0
182	766	5	2.7	34	0	0
198	838	3	1	43	0	0
140	592	2	0.5	32	0	0
159	671	6	1.8	26	0	0
167	702	8	2.3	25	0	0
146	615	5	1.5	25	0	0
147	619	4	1.1	29	0	0
138	583	2	0.6	30	0	0
158	665	6	1.8	26	0	0
148	623	4	1.1	28	0	0
163	684	7	2.3	25	0	0

FISH	AVERAGE PORTION g	GI	GL
Anchovies, canned in oil	10	L	L
Cod, baked	120	L	L
Cod, coated in batter, frozen, baked	180	H	M
Cod, coated in crumbs, frozen, fried	100	H	M
Cod, dried, salted, boiled	90	L	L
Cod, frozen, grilled	120	L	L
Cod, in batter, fried	180	H	M
Cod, in parsley sauce, frozen, boiled	170	M	L
Cod, poached	120	L	L
Cod, smoked, poached	120	L	L
Cod, steamed	120	L	L
Conger eel, grilled	115	L	L
Dogfish, in batter, fried	125	L	L
Eels, jellied	70	L	L
Eels, stewed	70	L	L
Haddock, grilled	120	L	L
Haddock, in batter, fried	120	H	M
Haddock, in crumbs, fried	120	H	M
Haddock, in crumbs, frozen, fried	120	H	M
Haddock, in flour, fried	120	H	M
Haddock, poached	120	L	L
Haddock, smoked, poached	150	L	L
Haddock, smoked, steamed	150	L	L
Haddock, steamed	120	L	L
Hake, grilled	100	L	L
Halibut, grilled	145	L	L
Halibut, poached	110	L	L
Halibut, steamed	110	L	L
Herring, grilled	119	L	L
Herring, in oatmeal, fried	119	L	L
Herring, pickled	90	L	L
Hoki, grilled	190	L	L
Kipper, baked	130	L	L

Unless otherwise stated, values for bottled and canned seafood are for drained weights. Dishes are homemade unless otherwise stated.

ENERGY kcal	ENERGY kJ	FAT g	SATURATED FAT g	PROTEIN g	CARBO- HYDRATE g	FIBRE g
28	117	2	0.4	3	0	0
115	490	1	0.4	26	Trace	0
380	1589	21	6.5	23	26	1.1
235	983	14	1.5	12	15	0.4
124	527	1	0.2	29	0	0
114	482	2	0.5	25	Trace	0
445	1856	28	7.4	29	21	0.9
143	598	5	3	20	5	0.2
113	475	1	0.4	25	Trace	0
121	511	2	0.7	26	Trace	0
100	420	1	0.2	22	0	0
158	660	6	Trace	25	0	0
369	1531	27	6.6	18	13	0.5
69	284	5	1.3	6	Trace	0
141	589	9	1.3	14	0	0
125	530	1	0.2	29	0	0
278	1163	17	4.4	21	12	0.5
209	875	10	0.8	26	4	0.2
235	986	12	1	18	15	0.7
166	698	5	0.5	25	5	0.2
136	572	5	3.1	21	1	0
201	843	9	5.6	28	2	0
152	644	1	0.3	35	0	0
107	454	1	0.1	25	0	0
113	478	3	0.4	22	0	0
175	744	3	0.6	37	0	0
169	713	6	3	27	1	0
144	608	4	0.6	26	0	0
215	900	13	3.3	24	0	0
278	1160	18	3.3	27	2	0.1
188	789	10	3.3	15	9	0
230	969	5	1	46	0	0
267	1112	15	2.3	33	0	0

FISH	AVERAGE PORTION g	GI	GL
Kipper, boil-in-the-bag, boiled, with butter added	170	L	L
Kipper, grilled	130	L	L
Lemon sole, goujons, baked	170	H	M
Lemon sole, goujons, fried	170	H	M
Lemon sole, grilled	109	L	L
Lemon sole, in crumbs, fried	109	H	M
Lemon sole, steamed	109	L	L
Lobster, boiled, dressed with shell	250	L	L
Mackerel, canned in brine	200	L	L
Mackerel, canned in tomato sauce	125	L	L
Mackerel, fried	161	L	L
Mackerel, grilled	147	L	L
Mackerel, smoked	150	L	L
Monkfish, grilled	70	L	L
Mullet, Grey, grilled	100	L	L
Mullet, Red, grilled	110	L	L
Pilchards, canned in tomato sauce	215	L	L
Plaice, frozen, grilled	165	L	L
Plaice, frozen, steamed	130	L	L
Plaice, goujons, baked	130	L	L
Plaice, goujons, fried	150	L	L
Plaice, grilled	130	L	L
Plaice, in batter, fried	200	H	M
Plaice, in crumbs, fried	150	H	M
Plaice, in crumbs, frozen, fried	150	H	M
Plaice, steamed	130	L	L
Red snapper, fried	102	L	L
Rock salmon, in batter, fried	125	H	M
Salmon, grilled	82	L	L
Salmon, pink, canned in brine, skinned and boned	100	L	L
Salmon, raw	100	L	L

Unless otherwise stated, values for bottled and canned seafood are for drained weights. Dishes are homemade unless otherwise stated.

ENERGY kcal	ENERGY kJ	FAT g	SATURATED FAT g	PROTEIN g	CARBO-HYDRATE g	FIBRE g
403	1673	30	2.7	34	Trace	0
332	1378	25	4	26	0	0
318	1318	25	Trace	27	25	Trace
636	2640	49	5.4	26	24	Trace
106	445	2	0.2	22	0	0
235	985	14	1.4	18	10	0.4
99	419	1	0.1	22	0	0
258	1088	4	0.5	55	Trace	0
474	1970	36	8	38	0	0
258	1070	19	4.1	20	2	Trace
438	1819	31	6.4	39	0	0
351	1461	25	5.1	31	0	0
531	2198	46	9.5	28	0	0
67	285	0	0.1	16	0	0
150	629	5	1.4	26	0	0
133	561	5	1.4	22	0	0
310	1292	17	3.7	36	2	Trace
200	843	3	0.5	42	0	0
120	506	2	0.3	25	0	0
395	1651	24	0	11	36	Trace
639	2657	48	5.4	13	41	Trace
125	525	2	0.4	26	0	0
514	2144	34	9	30	24	1
342	1427	21	2.3	27	13	0.3
261	1094	14	1.5	21	14	0.5
121	510	2	0.4	25	0	0
129	542	3	0.7	25	0	0
369	1531	27	6.6	18	13	0.5
176	735	11	2.1	20	0	0
153	644	7	1.3	24	0	0
180	750	11	1.9	20	0	0

FISH	AVERAGE PORTION g	GI	GL
Salmon, red, canned in brine, skinned and boned	100	L	L
Salmon, smoked	56	L	L
Salmon, steamed	77	L	L
Sardines, canned in brine	100	L	L
Sardines, canned in oil	100	L	L
Sardines, canned in tomato sauce	100	L	L
Sardines, grilled	40	L	L
Skate, grilled	215	L	L
Skate, in batter, fried	170	H	M
Sole fillets, raw	100	L	L
Sprats, fried	132	L	L
Swordfish, grilled	125	L	L
Trout, brown, steamed	155	L	L
Trout, rainbow, grilled	155	L	L
Tuna, canned in brine	45	L	L
Tuna, canned in oil	45	L	L
Tuna, canned in spring water	85	L	L
Tuna, raw	45	L	L
Whitebait, in flour, fried	80	L	L
Whiting, in crumbs, fried	162	L	L
Whiting, steamed	85	L	L

FISH PRODUCTS AND DISHES

Caviare, bottled in brine	19	L	L
Fish balls, steamed	50	L	L
Fish cakes, fried	100	M	M
Fish cakes, grilled	100	M	M
Fish cakes, salmon, grilled	100	M	M
Fish fingers, cod, fried	56	L	L
Fish fingers, cod, grilled	56	L	L
Fish paste	10	L	L
Fisherman's pie, shop bought	170	M	M

Unless otherwise stated, values for bottled and canned seafood are for drained weights. Dishes are homemade unless otherwise stated.

ENERGY kcal	ENERGY kJ	FAT g	SATURATED FAT g	PROTEIN g	CARBO-HYDRATE g	FIBRE g
167	700	8	1.7	22	0	0
80	335	3	0.4	14	0	0
152	634	10	1.8	15	0	0
172	721	10	2.8	22	0	0
220	918	14	2.9	23	0	0
162	678	10	2.8	17	1	Trace
78	326	4	1.2	10	0	0
170	725	1	0.2	41	0	0
286	1193	17	4.3	25	8	0.3
83	351	2	0.2	17.4	0	0
548	2268	46	7	33	0	0
174	729	6	1.5	29	0	0
209	877	7	1.6	36	0	0
209	876	8	1.7	33	0	0
45	190	1	0.1	11	0	0
85	357	4	0.7	12	0	0
109	456	3	0.7	20.1	0	0
61	258	2	0.5	11	0	0
420	1739	38	2.1	16	4	0.2
309	1298	17	1.8	29	11	0.3
78	331	1	0.1	18	0	0
17	73	1	0.2	2	0	0
37	157	0	0.9	6	3	0
218	912	14	1.4	8	16	0.6
154	650	5	0.6	10	20	0.6
273	1137	20	2.9	10	14	0.7
133	557	8	2	7	9	0.3
112	469	5	1.6	8	9	0.4
17	71	1	0.5	2	0	0
201	838	9	3.1	15	15	0.9

FISH PRODUCTS AND DISHES	AVERAGE PORTION g	GI	GL
Kedgeree	300	M	H
Mackerel pâté, smoked	40	L	L
Roe, cod, hard, coated in batter, fried	160	L	L
Roe, cod, hard, fried	116	L	L
Roe, herring, soft, fried	85	L	L
Salmon en croûte, shop bought	100	L	L
Taramasalata	45	L	L
Tuna pâté	40	L	L

SEAFOOD AND SHELLFISH			
Cockles, boiled	25	L	L
Cockles, bottled in vinegar	25	L	L
Crab, boiled, dressed with shell	130	L	L
Crab, canned in brine	40	L	L
Lobster, boiled, dressed with shell	250	L	L
Mussels, boiled and shelled	40	L	L
Mussels, canned or bottled without shells	40	L	L
Oysters, uncooked and shelled	120	L	L
Prawns, boiled and shelled	60	L	L
Scallops, steamed and shelled	70	L	L
Squid, in batter, fried	120	L	L
Whelks, boiled and shelled	30	L	L
Winkles, boiled and shelled	30	L	L

SEAFOOD PRODUCTS AND DISHES			
Crabsticks	100	M	L
Scampi, in breadcrumbs, frozen, fried	170	L	L
Seafood cocktail	88	L	L
Seafood pasta, shop bought	290	M	H

Unless otherwise stated, values for bottled and canned seafood are for
drained weights. Dishes are homemade unless otherwise stated.

ENERGY kcal	ENERGY kJ	FAT g	SATURATED FAT g	PROTEIN g	CARBO- HYDRATE g	FIBRE g
498	2103	24	6.9	43	32	Trace
147	608	14	2.5	5	1	Trace
302	1264	19	2.6	20	14	0.3
234	979	14	1.9	24	3	0.1
225	941	13	2.2	22	4	0.2
288	1202	19	3.1	12	18	0.3
227	935	24	1.8	1	2	Trace
94	393	7	3.1	7	0	Trace
13	57	1	0.1	3	Trace	0
15	63	1	0.1	3	Trace	0
166	696	7	0.9	25	Trace	0
31	130	0	0	7	Trace	0
258	1088	4	0.5	55	Trace	0
42	176	1	0.2	7	1	0
39	166	1	0.2	7	1	0
78	330	2	0.2	13	3	0
59	251	1	0.1	14	0	0
83	351	1	0.3	16	2	Trace
234	978	12	2.5	14	19	0.6
27	113	1	0.1	6	Trace	0
22	92	1	0.1	5	Trace	0
68	290	0	0	10	7	0
403	1685	23	2.4	16	35	0
77	325	1	0.3	14	3	0
319	1334	14	8.1	26	22	1.2

BURGER KING	AVERAGE PORTION g	GI	GL
Bacon and Egg Sandwich	139	H	H
Big King®	202	H	H
BK Chicken Flamer	162	H	H
BK Spicy Beanburger	239	H	H
Cajun Chicken Deli Wrap	208	H	H
Cheeseburger	129	H	H
Chicken Caesar Deli Wrap	208	H	H
Chicken Royale	210	H	H
Chicken Royale Club	241	H	H
Chicken Whopper	260	H	H
Chicken Whopper Junior	159	H	H
Chicken Whopper Lite	161	H	H
Double Cheeseburger	185	H	H
Double Cheeseburger with Bacon	195	H	H
Hamburger	117	H	H
Hash Browns, large	102	H	H
Hash Browns, medium	68	H	H
Kids Cheeseburger	120	H	H
Kids Hamburger	107	H	H
Kids Veggie Burger	165	H	H
King Fries, large	142	H	H
King Fries, regular	116	H	H
King Fries, small	74	H	M
Onion Rings, large	120	L	L
Onion Rings, regular	90	L	L
Sausage and Egg Sandwich	160	H	H
Sausage, Bacon and Egg Sandwich	182	H	H
Veggie Burger	223	H	H
Whopper®	267	H	H
Whopper Junior	151	H	H
Whopper Junior with Cheese	163	H	H
Whopper with Cheese	292	H	H
XL Double Whopper	348	H	H
XL Double Whopper with Cheese	373	H	H

ENERGY kcal	ENERGY kJ	FAT g	SATURATED FAT g	PROTEIN g	CARBO-HYDRATE g	FIBRE g
296	1153	13	3.7	15	30	2.7
540	2163	31.3	12.8	33.3	30.3	2.2
308	1295	12	2.3	20	30	3.1
505	2112	20	5.8	19	63	9.3
511	2146	27.5	3.9	18	48	3.1
331	1289	14	6.4	20	30	1.8
835	1682	25.5	3.9	18.3	45.5	3.0
638	2696	40	1.4	25	47	4.9
668	2823	42.1	2.4	26.9	47.7	5.3
548	2300	23.4	1.3	39.4	45	2.5
339	1425	13.9	0.7	24.3	29.3	1.7
289	1223	7.5	1.1	25	29.9	1.7
492	1961	26	12.4	33	30	2.1
509	2034	28.3	13.3	37.4	30.7	2.1
290	1120	11	4.2	17	30	1.8
318	1330	19.7	4.4	2.2	33.0	3.8
212	887	13	2.9	2	22	2.6
328	1276	14	6.4	19.4	29.9	1.7
287	1107	10.6	4.2	17	29.7	1.7
359	1512	11.1	1.1	11.9	52.8	7.1
490	2047	19.6	3.4	3.7	52.7	3.6
400	1672	16	2.8	3	43	2.9
259	1081	10.2	1.8	1.9	32.3	1.9
348	1458	16.7	1.9	5.8	43.7	4.6
261	1094	13	1.4	4	33	3.4
375	1481	19	5.5	20	32	3
430	1712	23.1	7.4	24.1	31.8	3.1
432	1818	17	3.5	15	55	7.6
646	2583	38	8.1	31	48	3.6
372	1475	19.6	4.4	17.4	30.6	2.1
413	1644	23	6.6	19.8	30.7	2.1
728	2921	44.7	12.5	35.4	47.9	3.6
873	3531	53.9	15.2	51.6	47.6	4.2
955	3869	60.7	19.6	56.4	47.9	4.2

KENTUCKY FRIED CHICKEN	AVERAGE PORTION g	GI	GL
BBQ Beans, large	320	M	M
BBQ Beans, regular	125	M	M
Cheese slice	59	L	L
Chicken drumstick (1)	72.5	L	L
Chicken Fillet Burger (with mayonnaise)	213.7	H	H
Chicken Fillet Burger (without mayonnaise)	213.7	H	H
Chicken Fillet Tower	247.9	H	H
Chicken Rib	110.61	L	L
Chicken Thigh	103.6	L	L
Chicken Wings	71.07	L	L
Coleslaw, large	200	L	L
Coleslaw, regular	99.32	L	L
Corn cobette (with butter)	65	L	L
Corn cobette (without butter)	65	L	L
Crispy Strips (1)	36.75	L	L
Fried chicken (2 pieces)	372	L	L
Fries, large	149.22	H	H
Fries, regular	114.8	H	H
Popcorn	100	M	L
Popcorn chicken, large	218	L	L
Popcorn chicken, regular	147	L	L
Twister (with pepper mayonnaise)	224.8	H	H
Twister (without pepper mayonnaise)	211.3	H	H
Zinger Burger	185.4	H	H
Zinger Burger with cheese slice	198.9	H	H
Zinger Tower Burger (with mayonnaise)	256.1	H	H
Zinger Tower Burger (without mayonnaise)	249.6	H	H

ENERGY kcal	ENERGY kJ	FAT g	SATURATED FAT g	PROTEIN g	CARBO-HYDRATE g	FIBRE g
294.4	1231.8	1.12	0.224	13.92	56.96	9.21
115	481.17	0.42	0.084	5.22	21.36	4.14
194.1	807	15.39	10.66	11.21	1.062	0
185	775	11.25	1.91	13.96	7.17	0.8
470.85	1976.02	19.6	3.06	31.99	41.52	3.38
408.94	1716	17.06	2.64	27.78	36.07	2.94
574.3	2406	27.82	5.6	27.78	49.02	3.6
292	1222	17.21	2.38	24.13	10.02	1.16
288	1199	20.35	4.27	19.92	5.8	0.87
574.3	2406	27.82	5.6	27.78	49.02	3.6
294	1212	26.9	1.6	1.86	10.92	2.66
146	606	13.45	0.8	0.93	5.46	1.33
68.68	290	1.69	0.76	2.13	11.27	1.40
79.7	336.96	1.5	0	2.66	14.77	3.05
113.23	472.92	6.37	0.98	7.63	6.11	0.61
1551	2305.43	23	3.8	28	14	0.8
382	1600	19.22	4.46	4.95	47.38	3.97
294	1232	14.78	3.43	3.81	36.44	3.06
264.5	1104.75	16.075	2.35	17.25	12.75	1.025
573.97	2397.31	35	4.95	37.5	27.62	1.06
388.82	1623.98	24	3.35	25.4	18.71	0.72
541.37	2262	30.02	6.26	23.5	43.88	4.14
499.51	2090	29.07	6.07	22.77	42.49	4.00
440	1847	19.33	2.89	25.49	41.05	2.56
490.60	2055.92	19.6	5.37	26.11	41.82	2.59
607.29	2546	31.24	6.65	30.99	50.62	3.17
555.51	2324.31	25.5	6.81	31.68	51.73	3.25

INDIAN	AVERAGE PORTION g	GI	GL
Chicken biryani	400	M	M
Chicken dhansak	350	L	L
Chicken dupiaza	350	L	L
Chicken jalfrezi	350	L	L
Chicken korma	350	L	L
Chicken tikka	350	L	L
Chicken tikka masala	350	L	L
Lamb balti	350	L	L
Lamb rogan josh	350	L	L
Meat samosas	70	L	L
Poppadoms	70	H	H
Prawn bhuna	400	L	L
Prawn madras	350	L	L
Vegetable balti	350	L	L
Vegetable biryani	350	M	M

ORIENTAL DISHES			
Aromatic crispy duck	125	L	L
Chicken chop suey	450	L	L
Chicken chow mein	350	M	H
Chicken fried rice	350	M	H
Chicken satay	170	L	L
Chicken with cashew nuts	360	L	L
Egg fried rice	270	M	H
Green chicken curry	350	L	L
Meat spring roll	55	L	M
Pancakes	70	M	H
Prawn crackers	70	L	M
Sesame prawn toasts	70	M	M
Spare ribs	340	L	L
Stir-fried beef with green peppers in black bean sauce	360	L	L
Stir-fried Thai vegetable curry	350	L	L

ENERGY kcal	ENERGY kJ	FAT g	SATURATED FAT g	PROTEIN g	CARBO-HYDRATE g	FIBRE g
651	2144	30	8.0	34	66	4.4
503	1509	30	6.0	40	21	6.7
397	1168	25	4.9	40	4	6.3
416	1203	27	5.3	34	11	7.0
668	1753	51	20.0	44	8	7.0
421	1470	15	5.6	71	Trace	1.0
551	1488	40	13.7	47	Trace	7.7
534	1518	35	8.8	43	11	6.7
510	1422	35	9.8	43	6	3.1
191	553	12	3.2	8	13	1.5
351	916	27	5.6	8	20	4.1
363	802	35	4.0	6	7	7.6
390	1042	29	3.5	27	6	7.0
373	983	28	5.3	8	23	7.7
467	1468	25	4.9	10	55	6.0
412	1107	30	9.1	35	15	1.1
363	1095	21	3.6	37	7	5.4
516	1662	25	4.2	30	46	3.9
562	1948	21	3.5	23	75	0.0
324	1006	18	4.9	37	5	3.7
470	1331	31	5.4	38	10	0.0
491	1809	13	1.6	12	87	2.2
417	1125	30	18.2	31	5	8.4
133	374	9	2.1	4	10	1.0
213	790	6	Trace	6	37	0.0
386	1061	27	2.6	0	37	0.8
268	699	21	2.7	9	12	1.3
873	2358	64	10.2	75	7	1.0
373	1158	20	5.0	38	11	6.5
351	882	29	13.7	13	11	9.1

ORIENTAL DISHES	AVERAGE PORTION g	GI	GL
Stir-fried vegetables	340	L	L
Sweet and sour chicken	300	L	L
Sweet and sour pork, battered	300	L	L
Szechuan prawns with vegetables	350	L	L

BURGERS AND HOTDOGS			
Cheeseburger, large, double	258	H	H
Cheeseburger, large, single	219	H	H
Cheeseburger, regular, double	228	H	H
Cheeseburger, triple, plain	304	H	H
Hamburger, large, double	226	H	H
Hamburger, large, single, with seasoning and sauce	172	H	H
Hamburger, large, triple patty, seasoning and sauce	259	H	H
Hamburger, regular, double, plain	176	H	H
Hamburger, regular, double, with seasoning and sauce	215	H	H
Hamburger, regular, single, plain	90	H	H
Hamburger, regular, single, with seasoning and sauce	106	H	H

MEXICAN DISHES			
Burrito, beans	217	L	L
Burrito, beans and cheese	186	L	L
Burrito, beans and chilli peppers	204	L	L
Burrito, beans and meat	231	L	L
Burrito, beans, cheese and beef	203	L	L
Burrito, beef	220	L	L
Burrito, beef and chilli peppers	201	L	L
Burrito, beef, cheese and chilli peppers	304	L	L
Chimichanga, beef	174	L	L

Unless otherwise specified, burgers include garnish, seasonings and sauce.

ENERGY kcal	ENERGY kJ	FAT g	SATURATED FAT g	PROTEIN g	CARBO-HYDRATE g	FIBRE g
177	455	14	2.4	6	7	6.1
575	1810	30	3.9	23	57	1.8
705	2115	42	6.9	23	63	3.0
297	912	16	1.8	27	11	4.9
704	2946	44	17.7	38	40	2.1
563	2354	33	15	28	38	2.1
650	2718	35	12.8	30	53	2.1
796	3332	51	21.7	56	27	2.1
540	2260	27	10.5	34	40	2.1
427	1785	21	7.9	23	37	2.1
692	2893	41	15.9	50	29	2.1
544	2276	28	10.4	30	43	2
576	2410	32	12	32	39	2.1
274	1148	12	4.1	12	31	2
272	1140	10	3.6	12	34	2.3
447	1871	13	6.9	14	71	1.5
378	1579	12	6.8	15	55	1.5
412	1724	15	7.6	16	58	1.5
508	2125	18	8.3	22	66	1.5
331	1384	13	7.1	15	40	1.5
524	2191	21	10.5	27	59	1.5
426	1783	17	8	22	49	1.5
632	2645	25	10.4	41	64	1.5
425	1777	20	8.5	20	43	1.5

MEXICAN DISHES

	AVERAGE PORTION g	GI	GL
Chimichanga, beef and cheese	183	L	M
Chimichanga, beef and chilli peppers	190	L	M
Chimichanga, beef, cheese and chilli peppers	180	L	M
Enchilada, cheese	163	M	M
Enchilada, cheese and beef	192	M	M
Enchilada, vegetable	360	M	M
Fajita, chicken, meat only	170	L	L
Nachos, cheese	113	M	M
Nachos, cheese and jalapeno peppers	204	M	M
Nachos, cheese, beans, ground beef and peppers	255	M	M

PIZZA

	AVERAGE PORTION g	GI	GL
Pizza, cheese and tomato, deep pan, shop bought	220	M	H
Pizza, cheese and tomato, deep pan	220	M	H
Pizza, cheese and tomato, French bread, frozen, shop bought	200	M	H
Pizza, cheese and tomato, frozen, shop bought	200	M	H
Pizza, cheese and tomato, thin base	116	M	H
Pizza, chicken, deep pan, shop bought	230	M	H
Pizza, fish topped, deep pan	230	M	H
Pizza, fish topped, thin base	150	M	H
Pizza, ham and pineapple, shop bought	200	M	H
Pizza, meat topped, deep pan	230	M	H
Pizza, meat topped, frozen, shop bought	200	M	H
Pizza, meat topped, thin base	150	M	H
Pizza, meat, deep pan, shop bought	230	M	H
Pizza, vegetable topped, deep pan	290	M	H
Pizza, vegetable topped, thin base	150	M	H

Unless otherwise specified, pizzas are takeaway.

ENERGY kcal	ENERGY kJ	FAT g	SATURATED FAT g	PROTEIN g	CARBO-HYDRATE g	FIBRE g
443	1854	23	11.2	20	39	1.5
424	1773	19	8.3	18	46	1.5
364	1521	18	8.4	15	38	1.5
319	1337	19	10.6	10	29	1
323	1350	18	9	12	30	1
525	1690	26	7.6	23	54	7.6
213	676	11	3.6	29	1	1.7
438	1208	31	11.6	18	24	3.4
608	2544	34	14	17	60	2
569	2379	31	12.5	20	56	2
471	1987	15	7.7	24	64	4.8
547	2310	16	11.4	27	77	4.8
461	1942	16	6.6	21	63	3.8
475	2002	18	9	23	60	3.8
322	1355	12	9.3	17	39	2.2
565	2382	19	7.8	31	72	4.8
507	2138	16	6.2	30	64	4.6
343	1446	12	9.2	20	41	2.8
521	2196	17	6.8	27	69	4.8
557	2345	21	14	30	67	4.6
496	2087	19	7.6	23	61	3.8
391	1642	18	7.5	21	39	2.8
624	2624	25	9.7	32	73	4.8
621	2624	18	7.8	32	88	4.9
332	1398	11	4.1	16	44	2.8

RICE, PASTA AND NOODLES	AVERAGE PORTION g	GI	GL
Basmati rice, cooked	180	M	H
Basmati rice, dry (2tbsp)	45	M	M
Brown rice, boiled	180	M	H
Brown rice, long-grain, dry (2tbsp)	185	M	M
Fettucine, cooked	100	L	H
Fettucine, dry	45	L	M
Gluten free pasta, cooked	100	M	M
Gluten free pasta, dry	55	M	M
Instant noodles	42	L	L
Jasmin rice, cooked	180	H	H
Jasmin rice, dry	45	H	H
Macaroni, boiled	230	M	M
Macaroni, wholemeal, boiled	230	M	M
Noodles, egg, boiled	230	L	L
Noodles, boiled	230	L	L
Noodles, fried	230	L	L
Red rice, boiled	230	M	M
Rice noodles, cooked	200	M	H
Rice noodles, dry	100	M	M
Risotto rice, cooked	150	M	H
Risotto rice, dry	45	M	M
Savoury rice, cooked	180	L	M
Spaghetti, boiled	220	L	L
Spaghetti, wholemeal, boiled	230	L	L
Udon noodles	114	H	H
Vermicelli, cooked	176	M	M
Vermicelli, dried	176	M	M
White rice, easy cook, boiled	180	M	H
White rice, fried in lard/dripping	300	M	H
White rice, glutinous, boiled	230	M	H
White rice, polished, boiled	230	M	H
Wild rice, cooked	164	M	H
Wild rice, dry	160	M	M

ENERGY kcal	ENERGY kJ	FAT g	SATURATED FAT g	PROTEIN g	CARBO-HYDRATE g	FIBRE g
247	1030	0.5	0	6.5	54.5	0
150	627	0.5	0	3	33	0.5
254	1075	2	0.5	5	58	1.4
41	171	0.3	0.1	0.9	8.5	1.6
93	388	0.4	0	3.2	18.3	0.9
156	652	0	0	3	36	0.5
345	1439	1	0.5	3	81	1.7
210	878	1.5	0.7	4	43	2
190	796	7	3.2	3.9	27.5	Trace
247	1031	0.6	Trace	5	54.2	0.2
156	652	1	Trace	3	36	0.2
198	840	1	0.2	7	43	2.1
198	840	1	0.2	7	43	6.4
143	607	1	0.2	5	30	1.4
143	607	1	0.2	6	30	1.6
352	1467	26	1	4	26	1.2
184	784	1	0.2	4	43	1.4
218	909	0	0	1.8	49.8	3.6
364	1523	1	0.2	3.4	83.2	1.6
210	876	0.6	0.1	4.4	46.6	Trace
161	672	0.2	0.1	2.9	35.6	Trace
256	1078	6	2	5	47	2.5
229	972	2	0.2	8	49	2.6
260	1116	2	0.2	11	53	8.1
113	472	0	0	5.8	24.4	Trace
192	803	0	0	1.6	43.8	Trace
641	2680	1	0.3	6.1	146.5	Trace
248	1057	2	0.5	5	56	0.2
393	1662	10	4.2	7	75	1.8
150	633	1	0.2	4	34	0.5
283	1201	1	0.2	5	68	0.5
166	694	1	0.1	6.5	35	3
571	2390	2	0.2	23.6	119.8	9.9

RICE AND PASTA DISHES

	AVERAGE PORTION g	GI	GL
Cannelloni, meat, shop bought	260	H	H
Cannelloni, spinach	340	H	H
Cannelloni, vegetable	340	H	H
Chicken risotto	340	H	H
Lasagne, meat, shop bought	420	H	H
Lasagne, spinach	420	H	H
Lasagne, spinach, wholemeal	420	H	H
Lasagne, vegetable	420	H	H
Lasagne, vegetable, wholemeal	420	H	H
Pasta with ham and mushroom sauce	235	M	M
Pasta with meat and tomato sauce	235	M	M
Peppers, stuffed with rice	175	M	H
Pilau, mushroom	180	M	H
Pilau, vegetable	180	M	H
Ravioli, cheese, cooked	200	L	M
Ravioli, meat, cooked	200	L	M
Ravioli, stuffed with cheese, tomato and herbs, shop bought	250	M	M
Ravioli, stuffed with meat and vegetables, shop bought	250	M	M
Rice and blackeye beans	200	H	H
Rice and blackeye beans, brown rice	200	H	H
Risotto, chicken	340	H	H
Risotto, vegetable, brown rice	290	H	H
Risotto, vegetable	290	H	H
Spaghetti bolognese, shop bought	400	M	M
Tortellini, cheese, cooked	200	L	M
Tortellini, meat, cooked	200	L	M
Tortellini, stuffed with cheese and ham, shop bought	250	M	M
Vine leaves, stuffed with rice	80	M	M

Unless otherwise stated, all dishes are homemade.

ENERGY kcal	ENERGY kJ	FAT g	SATURATED FAT g	PROTEIN g	CARBO-HYDRATE g	FIBRE g
315	1326	13	5.2	17	35	3.1
449	1880	26	7.8	15	43	2.7
493	2067	31	11.6	15	43	2.4
546	2310	10	4.5	31	84	Trace
601	2533	26	11.8	31	66	2.9
365	1541	13	5.5	15	53	4.6
391	1659	13	5.5	18	55	9.7
428	1810	18	9.2	17	52	4.2
445	1877	19	9.2	20	52	8.8
284	1194	14	8.2	13	27	2.1
263	1102	10	4	16	30	2
149	630	4	0.7	3	27	2.3
248	1048	8	4.5	4	43	0.7
248	1053	8	4.3	5	43	1
334	1396	14	9	12	40	3
342	1430	10	8	15	48	2
304	1267	13	7.9	17	30	0.6
324	1350	15	8.9	16	34	3.4
366	1556	7	3	12	68	2.8
350	1488	7	3	11	66	3.6
546	2310	10	4.5	31	84	Trace
415	1749	19	2.6	12	54	7
426	1798	19	2.9	12	56	6.4
432	1816	23	9.2	37	21	3.6
614	2568	14.5	7.2	27	94	3.8
404	1689	12	4	16	58	4
316	1318	9	6	16	44	1.4
210	875	14	2.1	2	19	1.0

BREAD, CAKES, SCONES & PASTRIES	AVERAGE PORTION g	GI	GL
Asian pastries	40	M	H
Bagel	70	H	H
Baguette	56	H	M
Banana loaf, homemade, no icing	85	M	H
Barley bread, sprouted	35	M	M
Battenburg cake	32	H	H
Brioche	45	M	M
Brown bread, sliced	36	M	L
Brown rolls/baps	48	M	L
Burfi	40	M	H
Carrot cake, homemade, no icing	85	M	H
Cheese-topped rolls/baps, white	85	M	H
Chelsea buns	78	M	H
Cherry cake	38	M	H
Chinese flaky pastries	40	M	H
Chocolate cake	40	M	H
Chocolate cake, with butter icing	65	M	H
Chocolate fudge cake	98	M	H
Choux buns	112	M	H
Ciabatta, plain	50	M	H
Coconut cake	40	M	H
Croissants	60	M	H
Crumpets	40	M	M
Currant buns	60	M	H
Custard tarts, individual	94	M	H
Danish pastries	110	M	H
Doughnuts, custard-filled	75	H	H
Doughnuts, jam	75	H	H
Doughnuts, ring	60	H	H
Doughnuts, ring, iced	75	H	H
Eccles cake	45	M	H
Eclairs, fresh	112	M	H
Fancy iced cakes, individual	30	M	H
Focaccia, herb/garlic and coriander	50	M	M

ENERGY kcal	ENERGY kJ	FAT g	SATURATED FAT g	PROTEIN g	CARBO-HYDRATE g	FIBRE g
215	897	16	8	3	17	0.8
191	831	1	0.3	7	40.5	1.7
140	585	0.5	Trace	5	30	1
230	968	9	5.6	4	35	1.5
77	320	0.5	0	3	15	1
118	496	6	1.5	2	16	0.4
144	607	4	2.8	4	24	1.0
75	317	1	0.2	3	15	1.3
113	482	2	0.3	5	22	1.8
117	487	8	4	5	7	0.8
349	1454	25	6.4	5	28	2.1
241	1016	7	3.4	9	38	1.2
285	1203	11	3.3	6	44	1.3
150	630	6	1.6	2	23	0.4
157	659	7	4	2	24	0.8
182	763	11	8.2	3	20	0.5
313	1306	19	14.3	4	33	0.8
351	1479	14	4.5	5	55	0.9
427	1766	36	19	6	20	0.8
135	574	2	0.3	5	26	1.2
174	726	10	2.6	3	20	1
224	938	12	5.9	5	26	1.0
83	352	1	0.2	3	18	0.8
178	750	5	2	5	32	1.6
260	1091	14	5.3	6	30	1.1
411	1728	16	6.2	6	56	1.8
269	1125	14	10.4	5	32	1.6
252	1061	11	3.2	4	37	1.6
238	997	13	3.8	4	28	1.4
287	1208	13	3.8	4	41	1.4
214	896	12	4.5	2	27	0.7
418	1746	27	14.3	5	42	0.6
122	515	3	2.8	1	21	0.4
147	620	4	0.6	5	26	0.7

BREAD, CAKES, SCONES & PASTRIES	AVERAGE PORTION g	GI	GL
French baguette, white	40	H	M
French baguette, white, part baked	40	H	M
French baton, granary	40	M	M
French stick/flute, white	40	H	M
Fruit buns, white, not iced	78	M	H
Fruit cake, plain	60	M	H
Fruit cake, rich	70	M	H
Fruit cake, rich, iced	70	M	H
Fruit cake, wholemeal	90	M	H
Garlic bread	20	H	M
Gingerbread	50	M	M
Gluten free bread (made with brown rice)	55	L	L
Granary bread, sliced	36	L	L
Granary rolls	56	L	L
Greek pastries	100	M	H
Gulab jamen/gulab jambu	40	M	H
Hamburger roll (small)	50	H	H
Hot cross buns	50	M	H
Jam tarts	34	M	H
Jam tarts, wholemeal	34	M	H
Jellabi	40	M	H
Madeira	40	M	H
Malt loaf, fruit	35	M	H
Milk bread, white	15	M	M
Mince pies, individual	55	M	H
Muffins, English, white	68	M	H
Muffins, English, white, toasted	68	M	H
Naan bread, garlic and coriander/plain	160	M	H
Pitta bread, white	75	M	L
Pitta bread, wholemeal	75	L	L
Pumpernickel bread	33	M	L
Rye bread with grains	45	M	L
Rye bread with seeds	45	M	L
Scones, cheese	48	H	H

ENERGY kcal	ENERGY kJ	FAT g	SATURATED FAT g	PROTEIN g	CARBO-HYDRATE g	FIBRE g
109	465	1	0.1	4	24	1.0
108	458	1	0.1	4	23	1.0
110	467	1	0.1	4	22	1.0
101	431	1	0.1	4	21	1.0
218	924	4	1.5	6	41	1.7
212	894	9	3.5	3	35	1.6
239	1007	8	2.4	3	42	1.2
249	1053	8	1.8	3	44	1.2
327	1373	14	4.3	5	48	2.2
73	306	4	1.9	2	9	1.0
190	799	6	1.9	3	32	0.6
110	460	2	0	2	21	2
87	369	1	0.3	4	18	1.3
133	565	2	0.3	6	24	2.0
322	1349	17	9	5	40	0.8
143	602	6	3	3	21	0.1
132	561	3	0.6	4.6	24.4	0.8
155	657	3	1	4	29	0.9
125	527	5	1.6	1	22	0.4
125	528	5	1.6	1	20	1.2
145	611	5	3	2	24	0.5
157	661	6	3.5	2	23	0.4
18	76	1	0.2	3	22.7	0.9
36	153	1	0.2	1	7	0.3
233	975	11	4.1	2	32	1.2
152	644	1	0.3	7	30	1.3
177	753	2	0.3	8	35	1.3
456	1929	12	1.6	12	80	3.2
191	813	1	0.7	7	41	1.8
199	845	1	0.4	6.9	43.4	3.9
67	283	1	0.1	2	15	2.1
103	431	1	0	3	22	3
104	435	1	0	3	22	3
174	731	9	4.9	5	21	0.8

BREAD, CAKES, SCONES & PASTRIES	AVERAGE PORTION g	GI	GL
Scones, fruit	48	H	H
Scones, plain	48	H	H
Scones, potato	57	H	H
Scones, wholemeal	50	H	H
Scones, wholemeal, fruit	50	H	H
Scotch pancakes	31	M	M
Slimmers white bread, sliced	20	M	M
Soda bread, brown	130	M	M
Sourdough bread	70	L	L
Soya bread (1 slice)	34	L	L
Sponge, fatless	58	L	M
Sponge, frozen	60	L	M
Sponge, jam-filled	60	M	H
Sponge, with butter icing	60	M	H
Swiss roll	30	M	H
Swiss rolls, chocolate, individual	30	M	H
Teacakes	55	M	H
Tortilla, soft, white	160	M	M
Tortilla wrap, white	51	L	L
Tortilla wrap, wholewheat	75	L	L
Waffles	65	M	H
Wheatgerm bread	30	M	M
White bread, crusty bloomer	35	H	M
White bread, farmhouse, large	35	H	M
White bread, farmhouse, small	27	H	M
White bread, premium	36	H	M
White bread, standard	36	H	M
White bread, standard, toasted	36	H	M
White bread with added fibre (small slice)	28	L	L
White rolls, crusty	50	H	M
White rolls, soft	45	H	M
Wholemeal bread	38	H	M
Wholemeal bread, toasted	38	H	M
Wholemeal rolls	48	H	M

ENERGY kcal	ENERGY kJ	FAT g	SATURATED FAT g	PROTEIN g	CARBO-HYDRATE g	FIBRE g
152	640	5	1.6	4	25	0.8
174	731	7	2.4	3	26	0.9
169	707	8	4.4	3	22	0.9
163	684	7	2.4	4	22	2.6
162	683	6	2	4	24	2.5
91	381	4	1.3	2	14	0.4
46	193	1	0.1	2	9	0.5
267	1132	4	1.0	11	50	4.9
190	794	0.5	0	7	38	2
81	339	2	0	6	11	4
171	722	4	1	6	31	0.5
190	795	10	3.1	2	24	0.4
181	768	3	1	3	39	1.1
294	1228	18	5.6	3	31	0.4
83	352	1	0.3	2	17	0.2
101	426	5	1.4	1	17	0.3
181	766	5	1.8	5	32	1.2
451	1903	14	2.9	12	73	3.0
146	613	3	0.7	4.4	25.3	1.2
220	920	5.4	0.8	6.3	37	3.6
217	911	11	4.7	6	26	1
66	281	1	0.2	3	12	1.2
86	368	1	0.2	3	18	0.8
83	353	1	0.2	3	17	0.7
66	281	1	0.2	2	14	0.7
83	352	1	0.2	3	17	0.7
79	335	1	0.1	3	17	0.7
97	414	1	0.1	3	21	0.0
60	251	0.5	0	3	12	2
131	558	1	0.3	5	27	1.2
114	485	1	0.3	4	23	0.9
82	349	1	0.2	4	16	1.9
102	431	1	0.2	5	20	0.0
117	498	2	0.2	5	22	2.1

CHEESE	AVERAGE PORTION g	GI	GL
Brie, without rind	40	L	L
Camembert	40	L	L
Cheddar, English, white	40	L	L
Cheddar, half-fat (15% fat)	40	L	L
Cheddar, vegetarian	40	L	L
Cheese spread	30	L	L
Cheshire, white	40	L	L
Cottage (4% fat)	40	L	L
Cottage, low-fat (1.5–2% fat)	40	L	L
Cream cheese	30	L	L
Cream cheese, fat free	30	L	L
Cream cheese, low fat	30	L	L
Danish Blue	30	L	L
Dolcelatte, without rind	40	L	L
Double Gloucester	40	L	L
Edam	40	L	L
Edam, half fat	40	L	L
Emmental	40	L	L
Feta	55	L	L
Fontina	28	L	L
Fromage frais, fruit	100	L	L
Fromage frais, fruit, virtually fat-free	100	L	L
Fromage frais, natural	100	L	L
Fromage frais, natural, virtually fat-free	100	L	L
Goats' milk	55	L	L
Gouda	40	L	L
Halloumi	40	L	L
Lancashire	40	L	L
Mascarpone	55	L	L
Monterey Jack	28	L	L
Mozzarella, fresh	55	L	L
Mozzarella, grated	55	L	L
Paneer	40	L	L
Parmesan, drums, freshly grated	20	L	L

Unless otherwise specified, generic cheeses are made with cows' milk.

ENERGY kcal	ENERGY kJ	FAT g	SATURATED FAT g	PROTEIN g	CARBO- HYDRATE g	FIBRE g
144	596	12	7.3	8	2	0
116	482	9	6.0	9	Trace	0
166	690	14	8.7	10	0	0
109	456	6	4.3	13	Trace	0
156	647	13	8.3	10	Trace	0
81	335	7	4.7	3	2	0
152	630	13	8.5	9	Trace	0
36	149	2	0.9	5	0	0
28	118	1	0.4	5	0	0
105	438	10	6.6	2.3	0.8	0
29	121	0	0.3	4.3	1.7	0
70	292	5.3	3.4	3.2	2.1	0
103	425	9	5.7	6	Trace	0
158	652	14	8.7	7	Trace	0
165	684	14	9.3	10	Trace	0
136	566	10	6.3	11	Trace	0
92	383	4	2.7	13	Trace	0
160	663	12	8.2	12	Trace	0
138	570	11	7.5	8.6	0.8	0
110	462	9	5.4	7	0	0
135	566	5.6	0.0	5.2	16.9	0.4
50	211	0.2	0.0	6.7	5.6	0.4
113	468	8.0	5.6	6.0	4.4	Trace
48	205	0.1	0.0	7.5	4.6	Trace
174	722	14	9.8	12	Trace	0
151	625	12	8.1	10	Trace	0
124	516	9	6.6	10	0	0
153	633	13	8.4	10	Trace	0
230	949	24	16.2	3	Trace	0
107	443	30	5.4	25	0	0
141	587	11	7.6	10	Trace	0
164	680	12	8.1	14	Trace	0
130	539	10	6.2	10	Trace	0
97	403	7	4.6	9	Trace	0

CHEESE	AVERAGE PORTION g	GI	GL
Pecorino	28	L	L
Port Salut	40	L	L
Processed cheese, slices	20	L	L
Provolone	28	L	L
Red Leceister	40	L	L
Ricotta	55	L	L
Romano	28	L	L
Roquefort	28	L	L
Soft white spreadable, low-fat (<10%)	30	L	L
Soft white spreadable, medium-fat (15%)	30	L	L
Soft white spreadable, full-fat	30	L	L
St Paulin	40	L	L
Stilton, blue	35	L	L
Wensleydale	40	L	L

CREAM AND SUBSTITUTES			
Cream, clotted	45	L	L
Cream, double	30	L	L
Cream, half	30	L	L
Cream, single	15	L	L
Cream, soured	30	L	L
Cream, whipping	30	L	L
Cream, frozen, whipping	30	L	L
Cream, sterilised, canned	45	L	L
Cream, UHT, canned spray	10	L	L
Cream, UHT, half-fat	15	L	L
Cream, UHT, single	15	L	L
Cream, UHT, whipping	30	L	L
Crème fraîche	50	L	L
Crème fraîche, low-fat	50	L	L
Mock cream, double	30	L	L
Mock cream, single	30	L	L
Mock cream, whipping	30	L	L

Unless otherwise specified, generic cheeses are made with cows' milk and cream is fresh.

ENERGY kcal	ENERGY kJ	FAT g	SATURATED FAT g	PROTEIN g	CARBO- HYDRATE g	FIBRE g
110	459	8	4.8	1	1	0
133	554	10	7.2	10	Trace	0
59	244	5	2.8	4	1	0
99	417	8	4.8	7	1	0
161	667	13	8.9	10	Trace	0
79	329	6	3.8	5	1	0
110	459	8	4.8	1	1	0
105	438	9	5.4	6	1	0
43	182	2	1.7	4	1	0
56	231	5	3.4	3	Trace	0
94	386	9	6.7	2	Trace	0
133	554	10	7.2	10	Trace	0
143	594	12	8.1	8	Trace	0
152	632	13	8.5	9	Trace	0
264	1086	29	17.9	1	1	0
135	555	16	9	1	1	0
44	184	4	2.5	1	1	0
30	123	3	1.8	0	1	0
62	254	6	3.8	1	1	0
112	462	12	7.4	1	1	0
114	468	12	7.5	1	1	0
108	443	11	6.7	1	2	0
31	127	2	2	0	0	0
21	86	2	1.2	0	1	0
29	122	3	1.8	0	1	0
112	462	12	7.4	1	1	0
190	792	20	13.2	1.2	1.4	0
85	355	7.5	4.5	1.8	2.5	0
136	561	11	8.7	1	1	0
57	236	4	4.2	1	1	0
96	395	9	8.4	1	1	0

EGGS

	AVERAGE PORTION g	GI	GL
Battery, raw	60	L	L
Boiled	50	L	L
Duck, boiled and salted	70	L	L
Duck, raw	75	L	L
Egg white	32	L	L
Egg yolk, raw	18	L	L
Free-range, raw	60	L	L
Fried in vegetable oil	60	L	L
Fried, without fat	50	L	L
Poached	50	L	L
Quail, raw	40	L	L

EGG DISHES

Omelette, cheese	150	L	L
Omelette, plain (two-egg)	120	L	L
Omelette, Spanish (two-egg)	150	L	L
Scrambled, with milk (two-egg)	120	L	L
Scrambled, without milk (two-egg)	100	L	L

MILK AND MILK SUBSTITUTES

Coffee whitener	3	L	L
Condensed milk, skimmed, sweetened	15	M	H
Condensed milk, whole, sweetened	15	M	H
Evaporated milk, reduced-fat	15	M	H
Evaporated milk, whole	15	M	H
Flavoured milk	214	L	L
Goats' milk, pasteurised	146	L	L
Semi-skimmed milk, pasteurised	146	L	L
Semi-skimmed milk, UHT	146	L	L
Sheep's milk	146	L	L
Skimmed milk, dried	3	L	L
Skimmed milk, dried, with vegetable fat	3	L	L

Unless otherwise specified, figures are for one egg, chicken's eggs are medium-sized and milk is cows' milk.

ENERGY kcal	ENERGY kJ	FAT g	SATURATED FAT g	PROTEIN g	CARBO-HYDRATE g	FIBRE g
88	367	1.9	6	8	Trace	0
74	306	1.5	5	6	Trace	0
139	575	2.7	11	10	Trace	0
122	510	2.2	9	11	Trace	0
12	49	Trace	Trace	2.9	Trace	0
61	252	1.6	5	3	Trace	0
86	358	1.7	7	7	Trace	0
107	447	2.4	8	8	Trace	0
87	363	1.8	6	8	Trace	0
74	306	1.5	5	6	Trace	0
60	252	1.2	4	5	Trace	0
399	1659	18.3	34	24	Trace	0
229	950	8.9	20	13	Trace	0
180	752	2.4	12	9	9	2.1
296	1230	13.9	27	13	1	0
160	664	3.3	12	14	Trace	0
16	68	1	1	0	2	0
40	171	0	0	2	9	0
50	211	2	0.9	1	8	0
18	77	1	0.2	1	2	0
23	94	1	0.9	1	1	0
146	614	3	1.9	8	23	0
88	369	5	3.4	5	6	0
67	285	2	1.5	5	7	0
67	283	2	1.6	5	7	0
139	578	8	5.5	8	7	0
10	44	0	0	1	2	0
15	61	1	0.5	1	1	0

MILK AND MILK SUBSTITUTES

	AVERAGE PORTION g	GI	GL
Skimmed milk, pasteurised	146	L	L
Skimmed milk, sterilised	136	L	L
Skimmed milk, UHT	146	L	L
Soya milk	146	L	L
Soya milk, flavoured	146	L	L
Whole milk, dried	3	L	L
Whole milk, pasteurised	146	L	L
Whole milk, sterilised	146	L	L
Whole milk, UHT	146	L	L

YOGHURTS

Crème fraîche (see under cream)			
Fromage frais (see under cheese)			
Drinking yoghurt	200	L	L
Probiotic yoghurt drink, orange	100	L	L
Probiotic yoghurt drink, plain	100	L	L
Yoghurt, French set, fruit, low-fat	125	L	L
Yoghurt, fruit	125	L	L
Yoghurt, fruit, low-fat	125	L	L
Yoghurt, fruit, virtually fat-free	125	L	L
Yoghurt, Greek-style, fruit, whole milk	150	L	L
Yoghurt, Greek-style, honey, whole milk	150	L	L
Yoghurt, Greek-style, natural, whole milk	150	L	L
Yoghurt, hazelnut, low-fat	125	L	L
Yoghurt, long life, fruit, whole milk	125	L	L
Yoghurt, natural, low-fat	125	L	L
Yoghurt, natural, virtually fat-free	125	L	L
Yoghurt, soya, fruit	125	L	L
Yoghurt, toffee, low-fat	125	L	L
Yoghurt, twin pot, fruit, virtually fat-free	135	L	L
Yoghurt, vanilla, low-fat	125	L	L

Unless otherwise specified, milk is cows' milk.

ENERGY kcal	ENERGY kJ	FAT g	SATURATED FAT g	PROTEIN g	CARBO-HYDRATE g	FIBRE g
48	204	1	0.1	5	7	0
44	188	1	0.1	5	7	0
47	200	1	0.1	5	7	0
47	193	2	0.4	4	1	Trace
58	245	2	0.3	4	5	Trace
15	62	1	0.5	1	1	0
96	402	6	3.5	5	7	0
96	404	6	3.5	5	7	0
96	402	6	3.5	5	7	0
124	526	Trace	Trace	6	26	Trace
67	279	0.9	0.6	1.5	13.4	1.3
68	284	1	0.7	1.7	13.1	1.4
103	435	1.4	1.0	4.3	19.5	0.3
133	564	3.8	2.5	4.9	21.4	0.3
97	412	1.4	0.9	5.1	17.1	0.3
75	318	0.5	0.0	5.9	12.5	0.3
205	857	12.6	8.4	7.2	16.8	Trace
221	927	12.5	8.4	7.7	21.0	Trace
198	824	15.3	10.2	8.4	7.2	Trace
111	469	1.9	0.8	5.5	19.1	0.3
125	529	4.3	0.0	3.9	19.1	0.3
69	294	1.3	0.9	5.9	9.3	Trace
67	286	0.3	0.0	6.6	10.3	Trace
92	388	2.3	0.3	2.9	16.0	0.4
114	484	1.1	0.8	4.8	22.6	Trace
55	236	0.1	0.1	4.5	9.7	0.7
114	484	1.1	0.8	4.8	22.6	Trace

FATS	AVERAGE PORTION g	GI	GL
Butter			
Butter	20	L	L
Ghee	7	L	L
Margarine			
Hard, animal and vegetable fats	10	L	L
Hard, vegetable fats	10	L	L
Soft, animal and vegetable fat	7	L	L
Soft, polyunsaturated	7	L	L
Other fats			
Compound cooking fat	15	L	L
Compound cooking fat, polyunsaturated	15	L	L
Dripping, beef	15	L	L
Ghee, vegetable	7	L	L
Lard	15	L	L
Suet, beef, shredded	15	L	L
Suet, vegetable	15	L	L
Spreads			
Blended 70% fat	7	L	L
Blended 40% fat	7	L	L
20–25% fat, not polyunsaturated	7	L	L
20–25% fat	7	L	L
35–40% fat	7	L	L
40% fat, not polyunsaturated	7	L	L
5% fat	7	L	L
60% fat	7	L	L
60% fat, with olive oil	7	L	L
70% fat	7	L	L
OILS			
Coconut oil	11	L	L
Corn oil	15	L	L
Grapeseed oil	11	L	L

ENERGY kcal	ENERGY kJ	FAT g	SATURATED FAT g	PROTEIN g	CARBO- HYDRATE g	FIBRE g
147	606	16	11	0	Trace	0
63	259	7	4.6	Trace	Trace	0
72	295	8	3.5	0	0	0
74	304	8	3.6	0	0	0
52	213	6	1.9	0	0	0
52	215	6	1.2	Trace	0	0
135	554	15	7.4	Trace	0	0
135	554	15	3.1	Trace	Trace	0
134	549	15	7.9	Trace	Trace	0
63	257	7	3.4	Trace	Trace	0
134	549	15	6	Trace	0	0
124	510	14	7.5	Trace	2	0.1
125	517	13	6.8	0	2	0
48	196	5	1.8	0	0	0
27	113	3	1.3	0	0	0
17	71	2	0.4	0	0	0
13	53	1	0.3	0	0	0
26	105	3	0.6	0	0	0
28	113	3	0.8	0	0	0
7	30	1	0.1	0	1	0.4
39	159	4	0.8	0	0	0
40	164	4	0.8	0	0	0
44	183	5	0.9	0	0	0
99	407	11	9.5	Trace	0	0
135	554	15	2.2	Trace	0	0
99	407	11	1.2	Trace	0	0

OILS	AVERAGE PORTION g	GI	GL
Hazelnut oil	2	L	L
Olive oil	11	L	L
Palm oil	11	L	L
Peanut oil	11	L	L
Rapeseed oil	11	L	L
Safflower oil	11	L	L
Sesame oil	3	L	L
Soya oil	11	L	L
Sunflower oil	11	L	L
Vegetable oil	11	L	L
Walnut oil	11	L	L
Wheatgerm oil	11	L	L

ENERGY kcal	ENERGY kJ	FAT g	SATURATED FAT g	PROTEIN g	CARBO-HYDRATE g	FIBRE g
99	407	11	0.9	Trace	0	0
99	407	11	1.6	Trace	0	0
99	407	11	5.3	Trace	0	0
99	407	11	2.2	Trace	0	0
99	407	11	0.7	Trace	0	0
99	407	11	1.1	Trace	0	0
27	111	3	0.4	Trace	0	0
99	407	11	1.7	Trace	0	0
99	407	11	1.3	Trace	0	0
99	407	11	1.1	Trace	0	0
99	407	11	1	Trace	0	0
99	407	11	2	Trace	0	0

SWEET SPREADS	AVERAGE PORTION g	GI	GL
Chocolate spread	16	L	L
Fruit spread	16	L	L
Honey	17	M	L
Lemon curd	15	M	L

SAVOURY SPREADS AND PÂTÉS

Fish paste	10	L	L
Mackerel pâté, smoked	40	L	L
Meat extract	9	L	L
Meat spread	10	L	L
Liver sausage	40	L	L
Pâté de foie gras	40	L	L
Pâté, chicken liver	40	L	L
Pâté, goose liver	40	L	L
Pâté, liver	40	L	L
Pâté, liver, tubed	40	L	L
Pâté, meat, reduced fat	40	L	L
Peanut butter, smooth	25	L	L
Peanut butter, crunchy	25	L	L
Sandwich spread	15	L	L
Tofu spread	45	L	L
Tuna pâté	40	L	L
Vegetable pâté	80	L	L
Yeast extract	9	L	L

JAMS AND MARMALADES

Jam, diabetic	15	L	L
Jam, fruit with edible seeds	15	L	L
Jam, reduced sugar	15	L	L
Jam, stone fruit	15	L	L
Marmalade	15	L	L
Marmalade, diabetic	15	L	L

Unless otherwise specified, spreads are made with polyunsaturated fats.

ENERGY kcal	ENERGY kJ	FAT g	SATURATED FAT g	PROTEIN g	CARBO-HYDRATE g	FIBRE g
91	380	6	0.9	1	9	0.2
19	83	Trace	Trace	0	5	0.1
49	209	0	0	0	13	0
42	180	1	0.2	0	9	0
17	71	1	0.5	2	0	0
147	608	14	2.5	5	1	Trace
16	68	0	0	4	0	0
19	80	1	0.6	2	0	Trace
90	377	7	2.1	5	2	0.3
185	773	18	5.8	4.6	1.9	Trace
80	336	5	1.6	5.4	2.6	Trace
185	773	18	5.8	4.6	1.9	Trace
128	534	11	3.8	5.7	0.6	Trace
114	472	10	3	5	0	Trace
76	319	5	1.4	7.2	1.2	Trace
156	645	13	2.9	6	3	1.4
152	628	13	2.4	6	2	1.5
28	117	1	0.2	0	4	0.1
94	349	9	1.3	2	1	0.2
94	393	7	3.1	7	0	Trace
138	574	11	6	6	5	2
16	69	0	0	4	0	0
26	109	0	0	0	9	0.1
39	167	0	0	0	10	0.1
18	78	Trace	Trace	0	5	0.1
39	167	0	0	0	10	0.1
39	167	0	0	0	10	0
26	109	0	0	0	9	0.1

BREAKFAST CEREALS	AVERAGE PORTION g	GI	GL
Bran cereal with fruit	55	M	H
Bran, flakes	30	H	M
Bran, strands	40	L	L
Bran, sultana	30	H	M
Bran, with oat and wheat	50	M	H
Corn flakes	30	H	H
Corn flakes, with nuts	30	H	H
Crunchy clusters with fruit	50	H	H
Crunchy clusters with chocolate	50	H	H
Frosted flakes	30	H	H
Fruit and fibre breakfast cereal	40	H	H
Hoops, honey	30	H	H
Hoops, honey and nut	30	H	H
Malted flakes	30	M	M
Muesli	50	M	L
Muesli, Swiss-style	50	M	L
Muesli, with extra fruit	50	M	L
Muesli, with no added sugar	50	M	L
Multigrain flakes	30	M	M
Oatmeal, quick cook, dry	15	M	M
Oatmeal, raw	15	L	L
Oat cereal with fruit and nuts	50	M	M
Oat cereal with tropical fruit	50	M	M
Oat clusters	30	M	M
Porridge, instant, made with water	180	M	M
Porridge, made with milk and water	160	L	L
Porridge, made with water	160	L	L
Porridge, made with whole milk	160	L	L
Puffed wheat	20	H	H
Rice pops	30	H	H
Rice pops, chocolate	30	H	H
Wheat, shredded	45	M	M
Wheat, shredded, honey and nut	40	M	H
Wholewheat biscuits	20	M	M

All values are without any sugar added.

ENERGY kcal	ENERGY kJ	FAT g	SATURATED FAT g	PROTEIN g	CARBO-HYDRATE g	FIBRE g
177	715	1.1	0.2	3.9	41.3	5
95	406	1	0.1	3	21	3.9
104	444	1	0.2	6	19	9.8
96	405	1	0.1	3	18	3.9
163	691	2	0.3	5	34	8.9
108	461	Trace	0	2	26	0.3
119	507	1	0.2	2	27	0.2
139	580	5	1.7	4	20	1.3
220	917	8	2.7	3	33	2.4
113	482	Trace	0	2	28	0.2
147	614	2	1.2	2	28	2.2
111	465	1	0.2	2	23	2.1
112	474	1	0.3	2	23	1.5
186	773	1	0.1	3	23	1.3
184	770	3	0.7	6	33	3.2
182	770	3	0.4	5	36	3.2
186	789	3	0.4	5	37	3.2
183	776	4	0.8	5	34	3.8
111	465	Trace	Trace	5	22	0.7
56	238	1	0.2	1.7	9.9	1.1
60	255	1	0.2	1.9	10.9	1
213	888	8	3	5	31	2
217	905	7	4	4	34	3
116	490	3	0.8	3	20	2.7
671	2844	14	2.2	21	123	13
133	557	5	2.3	5	18	1.3
78	334	2	0.3	2	14	1.3
186	781	8	4.3	8	22	1.3
64	273	Trace	0	3	13	1.1
111	472	0.1	0.1	2	27	0.2
115	491	0.1	0.1	2	28	0.2
150	630	1	0.2	5	30	5.2
152	642	3	0.9	4	28	4.1
70	300	0.1	0.1	2	15	1.9

SAVOURY BISCUITS	AVERAGE PORTION g	GI	GL
Cheese sandwiches	24	M	M
Cream crackers	14	M	M
Oatcakes, shop bought	26	M	M
Rye crackers	50	M	L
Taco shells (large)	21	L	L
Water biscuits	16	M	M
Wholemeal crackers	20	M	M

CRISPBREADS			
Breadsticks (4)	28	H	H
Crispbakes	16	H	H
Crispbread, rye	20	M	L
French toast	16	H	M
Matzos	20	H	M
Melba toast	6	H	M
Rice cakes	16	H	H

SWEET BISCUITS			
All-butter biscuits	19	M	M
Bourbon creams	28	M	M
Brandy snaps	30	M	M
Chocolate, full-coated	50	M	M
Chocolate-covered teacakes	26	M	M
Coconut biscuits	40	M	M
Cookies, chocolate chip	22	M	M
Cookies, chocolate chip and hazelnut (1)	24	M	M
Cookies, Danish butter	22	M	M
Cookies, stem ginger	32	M	M
Crunch biscuits	27	M	M
Custard creams	24	M	M
Custard creams, reduced fat	24	M	M

Unless otherwise specified, a helping is two biscuits.

ENERGY Kcal	ENERGY kJ	FAT g	SATURATED FAT g	PROTEIN g	CARBO-HYDRATE g	FIBRE g
123	516	5	3.5	1	17	0.2
62	260	2	0.4	1	10	0.3
115	482	4	1	3	16	1.3
183	766	1	0.1	4	41.1	1.7
98	411	5	0.7	1.5	13.1	1.3
70	297	1	Trace	2	12	0.5
83	349	2	1	2	14	0.9
108	464	4	1.6	4	20	0.8
60	250	Trace	Trace	2	12	0.6
64	273	0.1	0.1	2	14	2.3
63	262	1	0.5	2	12	0.5
77	327	0	0	2	17	0.6
23	94	Trace	Trace	1	4	0.3
56	234	Trace	Trace	2	12	0.8
90	378	4	3.4	Trace	14	0.2
136	566	6	3.6	2	20	0.6
131	550	6	3	1	19	0.2
262	1099	13	8.4	3	34	1
116	438	4	2.2	2	16	0.4
202	846	12	6	2	21	2
112	461	6	2.7	1	14	0.4
120	504	6	2.6	2	14	0.4
112	461	5	4	1	14	0.3
157	653	9	1.9	1	20	0.6
135	562	7	3.5	2	17	0.6
122	508	6	3.6	2	16	0.4
114	472	4	2.6	2	18	0.4

SWEET BISCUITS

	AVERAGE PORTION g	GI	GL
Digestives, chocolate, half coated	26	H	H
Digestives, milk chocolate, reduced fat	34	H	H
Digestives, plain	26	M	H
Digestives, reduced fat	28	M	H
Flapjacks (1 piece)	70	M	M
Gingernuts	20	M	M
Gluten free cookies (1)	14	L	L
Jaffa cakes®	26	M	M
Jam rings	38	M	M
Jam sandwich creams	30	M	M
Malted milk	16	M	M
Malted milk creams	26	M	M
Marshmallow teacakes, chocolate-coated	28	M	M
Morning coffee	10	M	M
Museli bar, plain	28	M	H
Nice	20	M	M
Nice creams	28	M	M
Rich tea	14	M	M
Tea biscuits	28	M	M
Shortbread	26	M	M
Shortbread, chocolate chip	40	M	M
Shortbread, reduced sugar (1)	33	M	M
Snowballs	42	M	M
Wafers, filled	14	M	M

Unless otherwise specified, a helping is two biscuits.

ENERGY kcal	ENERGY kJ	FAT g	SATURATED FAT g	PROTEIN g	CARBO-HYDRATE g	FIBRE g
128	538	6	3.2	2	17	0.6
158	660	10	6	2	24	0.6
122	514	5	2.2	2	18	0.6
130	542	6	2	2	20	1
339	1420	19	5.3	3	42	1.9
91	385	3	1.4	1	16	0.3
45	188	2.5	0	1	9	0.5
94	398	3	0.6	1	18	0.4
171	715	6	2.7	2	27	0.6
142	592	6	3.2	2	20	0.6
78	324	3	1.8	1	11	0.3
130	542	6	3.7	2	17	0.4
126	525	5	3	1	18	0.4
45	188	1	0.6	1	7	0.2
132	552	6	0.7	2.8	18	2
94	393	4	2.3	1	12	0.3
140	584	6	3.2	2	18	0.6
64	270	2	1.1	1	10	0.2
125	522	4	1	1.9	20.7	0.3
129	543	7	4.5	2	17	0.5
206	858	10	8.6	2	24	0.6
156	652	9	5.9	2	18	0.5
196	814	10	9.8	2	24	2.2
75	314	4	2.6	1	9	0.3

SAVOURY SNACKS	AVERAGE PORTION g	GI	GL
Bacon streaks	25	M	M
Bombay mix	30	M	M
Breadsticks	28	M	M
Cheese and potato puffs	27	M	M
Cheese balls	33	M	M
Corn chips (large bag)	100	L	M
Corn snacks	28	M	M
Oriental mix	50	M	M
Popcorn, candied	75	M	M
Popcorn, salted	75	L	L
Pork scratchings	22	M	M
Potato and corn sticks	19	M	M
Potato and corn, waffle-shaped snacks	50	M	M
Potato crisps	30	M	M
Potato crisps, crinkle cut	40	M	M
Potato crisps, jacket	40	M	M
Potato crisps, low-fat	30	M	M
Potato crisps, square	25	M	M
Potato crisps, thick, crinkle cut	40	M	M
Potato crisps, thick cut	40	M	M
Potato rings	30	M	M
Prawn crackers	20	M	M
Pretzels	30	H	H
Punjabi puri	35	M	M
Tortilla chips	50	M	M
Trail mix	25	M	M
Twiglets	25	M	M
Wheat crunchies	35	M	M

ENERGY kcal	ENERGY kJ	FAT g	SATURATED FAT g	PROTEIN g	CARBO-HYDRATE g	FIBRE g
113	473	5	1.6	2	16	0.5
151	630	10	1.2	6	11	1.9
108	464	4	1.6	4	20	0.8
140	585	9	3.2	2	15	0.3
148	621	8	1.8	2	19	0.8
1067	4449	67.3	9.2	13.4	115	6
141	591	9	3.8	1	16	1
273	1142	20	3	10	17	0.3
360	1514	14	1.5	2	58	1
445	1851	32	3.2	5	37	1
133	554	10	3.6	11	0	0.1
88	368	4	1.3	1	11	0.6
241	1009	12	2.8	2	32	1.3
159	665	10	4.2	2	16	1.6
219	913	14	5.8	2	22	2.3
204	851	13	5.3	3	21	1.9
137	577	6	2.8	2	19	1.8
108	454	5	2.2	2	14	1.1
203	848	12	5	2	22	1.6
200	836	11	4.6	3	23	1.6
157	656	10	4.2	1	18	0.8
103	432	7	1.9	0	11	0.3
114	479	1	0.2	3	24	0.8
188	784	12	2.9	3	18	0.9
230	964	11	2	4	30	3
108	451	7	1.3	2	9	1.1
96	404	3	1.2	3	16	2.6
158	662	7	3.2	4	21	1.2

	AVERAGE PORTION g	GI	GL
FLOUR			
Chapati, brown	100	M	L
Chapati, white	100	M	L
Cornflour	30	M	L
Rye, whole	20	L	L
Wheat, brown	100	M	L
Wheat, white, breadmaking	100	M	L
Wheat, white, plain	100	M	L
Wheat, white, self-raising	100	M	L
Wheat, wholemeal	100	M	L
GRAVY AND STOCK CUBES			
Instant granules	5	L	L
Instant granules, made up	45	L	L
Stock cubes, beef/chicken	7	L	L
Stock cubes, vegetable	7	L	L
BAKING INGREDIENTS			
Baking powder	4	L	L
Marzipan, shop bought	25	M	L
Mincemeat	28	M	L
Mincemeat, vegetarian	28	M	L
Yeast, bakers', compressed	5	L	L
Yeast, dried	5	L	L
MISCELLANEOUS			
Bran, wheat	7	M	L
Buckwheat, cooked	98	M	H
Buckwheat, dry	45	M	M
Bulgur, cooked	182	M	M
Bulgur, dry	45	M	M
Capers, canned	8.6	L	L

ENERGY kcal	ENERGY kJ	FAT g	SATURATED FAT g	PROTEIN g	CARBO-HYDRATE g	FIBRE g
333	1419	1	0.2	12	74	6
335	1426	1	0.1	10	78	3
106	452	0	0	0	28	0
67	286	1	0.1	2	15	2.3
323	1377	2	0.2	13	69	6.4
341	1451	1	0.2	12	75	3.1
341	1450	1	0.2	9	78	3.1
330	1407	1	0.2	9	76	3.1
310	1318	2	0.3	13	64	9
23	96	2	Trace	0	2	Trace
15	64	1	Trace	0	1	Trace
17	69	1	Trace	1	1	0
18	74	1	Trace	1	1	Trace
7	28	0	0	0	2	0
101	426	3	0.3	1	17	0.5
77	326	1	Trace	0	17	0.4
85	359	4	Trace	0	12	0.4
3	11	0	0	1	0	Trace
8	36	0	0	2	0	Trace
14	61	1	0.1	1	2	2.5
92	385	0.6	0.1	3.4	19.9	2.7
154	642	1.6	0.3	6	32.2	4.5
151	632	0	0.1	5.6	33.8	4
154	642	0.6	0.1	5.5	34.1	4.3
2	8	0	0	0.2	0.4	0.3

MISCELLANEOUS	AVERAGE PORTION g	GI	GL
Channa dahl	100	L	L
Coconut, creamed block	25	L	L
Coconut, desiccated	28	L	L
Couscous, cooked	157	M	L
Couscous, dry	173	M	M
Custard powder	30	L	L
Gelatine	3	L	L
Millet, cooked	174	H	H
Millet, raw	200	H	H
Olives, in brine, stoned	18	L	L
Pearl barley, dry	60	L	M
Pearl barley, raw	20	L	L
Quinoa, cooked	120	L	L
Quinoa, dry	100	L	L
Salt	5	L	L
Tomatoes, sundried, bottled in oil	10	L	L
Vinegar	15	L	L
Wheatgerm	5	M	L
Whey protein isolate (1 scoop)	28	L	L

PURÉES			
Tomato purée	20	L	L
Vegetable purée	20	L	L

SUGARS, SYRUPS AND TREACLE			
Jaggery	16	M	L
Sugar, brown	20	M	L
Sugar, Demerara	20	M	L
Sugar, icing	20	M	L
Sugar, white	20	M	L
Syrup, golden	55	M	L
Syrup, golden, pouring	50	M	L

ENERGY kcal	ENERGY kJ	FAT g	SATURATED FAT g	PROTEIN g	CARBO-HYDRATE g	FIBRE g
97	406	5	0	5.3	9.5	4.8
167	690	17	14.8	2	2	2
169	698	17	15	2	2	3.8
176	736	0	0	6	36.5	0.1
650	2721	1	0.2	22.1	134	3.1
106	452	0	0	0	28	0
10	43	0	0	3	0	0
207	867	2	0.3	6.1	41.2	2.3
756	3164	8	1.4	22	145.7	17
19	76	2	0.3	0	Trace	0.5
72	306	0	0	1.6	16.6	3
72	307	0	0	1.6	16.7	3.1
128	535	4	0	6	17	4
309	1311	5	0.5	13.8	55.7	5.9
0	0	0	0	0	0	0
50	204	5	0.7	0	1	0.5
3	13	0	0	0	0	0
18	75	0	0.1	1	2	0.8
115	481	1.5	0.1	24	1	0
15	65	Trace	Trace	1	3	0.6
14	51	1	0	1	1	0.6
59	250	0	0	0	16	0
72	309	0	0	0	20	0
79	336	0	0	0	21	0
79	336	0	0	Trace	21	0
79	336	0	0	Trace	21	0
164	698	0	0	0	43	0
148	632	0	0	Trace	40	0

	AVERAGE PORTION g	GI	GL
SUGARS, SYRUPS AND TREACLE			
Syrup, maple	55	M	L
Treacle, black	50	M	L
NUTS AND SEEDS			
Almonds, toasted	13	L	L
Barcelona nuts	15	L	L
Brazil nuts	10	L	L
Cashew nuts, plain	10	L	L
Cashew nuts, roasted and salted	25	L	L
Chestnuts	50	L	L
Coconut, fresh	28	L	L
Hazelnuts	10	L	L
Macadamia nuts, salted	10	L	L
Melon seeds	15	H	L
Mixed nuts	40	L	L
Mixed nuts and raisins	40	M	L
Peanuts, dry roasted	40	L	L
Peanuts, plain	13	L	L
Peanuts, roasted and salted	25	L	L
Pecan nuts	60	L	L
Pine nuts	5	L	L
Pistachio nuts, roasted and salted	10	L	L
Pumpkin seeds	16	L	L
Sesame seeds	12	L	L
Sunflower seeds	16	L	L
Walnuts	20	L	L

ENERGY kcal	ENERGY kJ	FAT g	SATURATED FAT g	PROTEIN g	CARBO-HYDRATE g	FIBRE g
144	602	Trace	Trace	0	37	0
129	548	0	0	1	34	Trace
81	334	7	0.6	3	1	1
96	396	10	2.3	2	1	1
68	281	7	1.6	1	0	0.4
57	237	5	1	2	2	0.3
153	633	13	2.5	5	5	0.8
85	360	1	0.3	1	18	2
98	405	10	8.7	1	1	2
65	269	6	0.5	1	1	0.7
75	308	8	1.1	1	0	0.5
87	363	7	1.8	4	1	0.8
243	1006	22	3.4	9	3	2.4
192	802	14	2.2	6	13	1.8
236	976	20	3.6	10	4	2.6
73	304	6	1.1	3	2	0.8
151	623	13	2.4	6	2	1.5
413	1706	42	3.4	6	3	2.8
34	142	3	0.2	1	0	0.1
60	249	6	0.7	2	1	0.6
91	378	7	1.1	4	2	0.8
72	296	7	1	2	0	0.9
96	400	8	0.8	3	3	1
138	567	14	1.1	3	1	0.7

TABLE SAUCES	AVERAGE PORTION g	GI	GL
Apple sauce, homemade	20	L	L
Brown sauce	20	L	L
Brown sauce, hot	20	L	L
Brown sauce, sweet	20	L	L
Chilli sauce	25	L	L
Horseradish sauce	20	L	L
Mint sauce	10	L	L
Mustard, powder, made up	8	L	L
Mustard, smooth	2	L	L
Mustard, wholegrain	14	L	L
Soy sauce, dark, thick	5	L	L
Soy sauce, light, thin	5	L	L
Tartare sauce	30	L	L
Tomato ketchup	20	L	L
WHITE SAUCES			
Bread sauce, made with semi-skimmed milk	45	M	M
Bread sauce, made with whole milk	45	M	M
Cheese sauce, made with semi-skimmed milk	62	M	M
Cheese sauce, made with whole milk	62	M	M
Onion sauce, made with semi-skimmed milk	62	M	M
Onion sauce, made with whole milk	62	M	M
White sauce, savoury, made with semi-skimmed milk	62	M	M
White sauce, savoury, made with whole milk	62	M	M
White sauce, sweet, made with semi-skimmed milk	62	M	M
White sauce, sweet, made with whole milk	62	M	M

ENERGY kcal	ENERGY kJ	FAT g	SATURATED FAT g	PROTEIN g	CARBO-HYDRATE g	FIBRE g
13	55	0	0	0	3	0.2
20	84	Trace	Trace	0	5	0.1
24	102	Trace	Trace	0	6	0.1
20	84	Trace	Trace	0	4	0.1
20	84	Trace	Trace	0	4	0.3
31	128	2	0.2	1	4	0.5
10	43	Trace	Trace	0	2	0.2
18	75	1	0.1	1	0	0
3	12	0	0	0	0	0
20	82	1	0.1	1	5	Trace
3	13	0	0	0	6	0.2
3	13	Trace	Trace	0	1	0.7
90	372	7	0.5	0	0	0.2
23	98	Trace	Trace	0	1	0.7

ENERGY kcal	ENERGY kJ	FAT g	SATURATED FAT g	PROTEIN g	CARBO-HYDRATE g	FIBRE g
42	177	1	0.6	2	6	0.1
50	208	2	1.2	2	6	0.1
112	465	8	3.9	4	6	0.1
122	508	8	4.8	4	6	0.1
53	224	3	1.1	2	5	0.2
61	257	4	1.7	2	5	0.2
79	334	5	1.8	3	7	0.1
93	387	6	2.7	3	7	0.1
93	393	4	1.7	2	12	0.1
105	441	6	2.5	2	12	0.1

CHUTNEYS	AVERAGE PORTION g	GI	GL
Chutney, apple, homemade	33	M	M
Chutney, mango, oily	33	M	M
Chutney, mango, sweet	33	M	M
Chutney, mixed fruit	33	M	M
Chutney, tomato	33	M	M
DIPS			
Dips, sour-cream-based	30	L	L
Guacamole	45	L	L
Hummus	30	L	L
Taramasalata	45	L	L
Tzatziki	45	L	L
DRESSINGS			
Blue cheese	25	M	M
'Fat-free'	15	L	L
French	15	L	L
Low-fat	15	L	L
Oil and lemon	15	L	L
Thousand island	30	L	L
Thousand island, reduced-calorie	30	L	L
Yogurt-based	30	L	L
MAYONNAISE AND SALAD CREAM			
Mayonnaise	30	L	L
Mayonnaise, homemade, made with lemon juice	30	L	L
Mayonnaise, homemade, made with vinegar	30	L	L
Mayonnaise, reduced-calorie	30	L	L

ENERGY kcal	ENERGY kJ	FAT g	SATURATED FAT g	PROTEIN g	CARBO-HYDRATE g	FIBRE g
66	283	Trace	Trace	0	17	0.4
94	397	4	Trace	0	16	0.3
62	266	Trace	Trace	0	16	0.3
51	219	Trace	Trace	0	13	0.3
42	179	Trace	Trace	0	10	0.4
108	445	11	3.7	1	1	Trace
58	239	6	1.2	1	1	1.1
56	234	4	0.5	2	3	0.7
227	935	24	1.8	1	2	Trace
30	124	2	1.3	2	1	0.1
114	472	12	6.2	1	2	0
10	42	0	0	0	2	0
69	285	7	0.6	0	1	0
11	45	1	0.1	0	1	Trace
97	399	11	1.1	0	0	Trace
97	401	9	0.9	0	4	0.1
59	243	5	0.5	0	4	Trace
88	363	8	0.8	1	3	Trace
207	853	23	3.3	0	1	0
237	974	26	3.8	1	0	Trace
217	894	24	3.5	1	0	0
86	356	8	1.1	0	2	0

MAYONNAISE AND SALAD CREAM	AVERAGE PORTION g	GI	GL
Salad cream	20	L	L
Salad cream, reduced-calorie	20	L	L

PICKLES			
Gherkins, pickled	25	L	L
Onions, pickled	30	L	L
Piccalilli	40	L	L
Pickle, chilli, oily	15	L	L
Pickle, chow chow, sour	15	L	L
Pickle, chow chow, sweet	15	L	L
Pickle, lime, oily	15	L	L
Pickle, mango, oily	15	L	L
Pickle, mixed vegetables	15	L	L
Pickle, sweet	15	L	L

COOKING SAUCES			
Barbecue sauce	25	L	L
Black bean sauce	20	L	L
Chilli sauce	25	L	L
Cook-in-sauces, canned, different flavours	150	L	L
Curry sauce, canned	150	L	L
Oyster sauce	15	L	L
Sauce, curry, sweet	150	L	L
Sauce, curry, tomato and onion	150	L	L
Soy sauce, dark, thick	5	L	L
Soy sauce, light, thin	5	L	L
Tomato sauce	90	L	L
Pasta sauce, tomato based	170	L	L

ENERGY kcal	ENERGY kJ	FAT g	SATURATED FAT g	PROTEIN g	CARBO-HYDRATE g	FIBRE g
70	288	6	0.8	0	3	0
39	161	3	0.5	0	2	0
4	15	Trace	Trace	0	1	0.3
7	30	Trace	Trace	0	1	0.4
34	144	0	0	0	7	0.4
41	168	4	Trace	0	1	0.2
4	18	0	0	0	1	0.2
17	73	0	0	0	4	0.2
27	111	2	Trace	0	1	0.2
27	110	2	Trace	0	1	0.2
3	14	0	0	0	1	0.2
21	91	0	Trace	0	5	0.2
23	99	0	0	0	6	0.1
19	79	0	0	1	2	0.4
20	84	Trace	Trace	0	4	0.3
65	272	4	0.2	2	12	Trace
117	486	8	0.4	2	11	Trace
12	51	0	Trace	1	3	Trace
137	570	8	2.3	2	14	2.1
297	1229	29	3	3	9	1.7
3	13	0	0	0	0	00
3	13	0	0	0	0	0
80	337	5	1.6	2	8	1.3
80	340	3	0.3	3	12	2.5

CUSTARDS	AVERAGE PORTION g	GI	GL
Crème caramel	90	L	L
Custard, canned, ready-to-serve	120	L	L
Custard, canned, ready-to-serve, low-fat	120	L	L
Custard, chilled, ready-to-serve	120	L	L
Custard, confectioners'	150	L	L
Custard, made with semi-skimmed milk	150	L	L
Custard, made with whole milk	120	L	L

ENERGY Kcal	ENERGY kJ	FAT g	SATURATED FAT g	PROTEIN g	CARBO-HYDRATE g	FIBRE g
98	416	1	Trace	3	19	Trace
118	497	3	2.3	3	20	0.0
93	395	2	0.0	3	18	0.0
135	569	6	4.4	3	18	0.0
255	1077	9	4.1	10	37	0.3
141	605	3	1.8	6	25	Trace
140	594	5	3.4	4	20	Trace

PASTRY	AVERAGE PORTION g	GI	GL
Cheese	100	H	H
Choux	100	H	H
Flaky	100	H	H
Shortcrust	100	H	H
Wholemeal	100	H	H

PASTRY DISHES	AVERAGE PORTION g	GI	GL
Beef pie, shop bought	141	M	M
Chicken and mushroom pie, single crust	100	L	L
Chicken pie, individual, baked	130	L	L
Cornish pasty	155	M	M
Cornish pasty, shop bought	155	M	M
Lamb samosa, baked	70	M	M
Lamb samosa, deep-fried	70	M	M
Pasty, vegetable	155	L	M
Pasty, vegetable, wholemeal	155	L	M
Pork and egg pie	60	M	M
Pork pie	60	M	M
Pork pie, mini	50	M	M
Quiche, broccoli	140	L	M
Quiche, broccoli, wholemeal	140	L	M
Quiche, cauliflower cheese	140	L	M
Quiche, cauliflower cheese, wholemeal	140	L	M
Quiche, cheese and egg	140	L	L
Quiche, cheese and egg, wholemeal	140	L	M
Quiche, cheese and mushroom	140	L	M
Quiche, cheese and mushroom, wholemeal	140	L	M
Quiche, cheese, onion and potato	140	M	M
Quiche, cheese, onion and potato, wholemeal	140	M	M
Quiche, mushroom	140	L	M

Unless otherwise specified, all pastry dishes are homemade.

ENERGY kcal	ENERGY kJ	FAT g	SATURATED FAT g	PROTEIN g	CARBO-HYDRATE g	FIBRE g
500	2083	34	15.3	13	37	1.5
325	1355	20	15	9	30	1.2
560	2332	41	14.7	6	46	1.8
521	2174	32	11.7	7	54	2.2
499	2080	33	11.8	9	45	6.3
437	1826	24	11.8	12	38	0.7
200	836	10	4.5	13	14	0.6
374	1563	21	9.1	12	32	1
456	1905	28	9.8	10	43	2.6
414	1731	25	9.1	10	39	1.4
187	781	10	2.5	8	16	1.2
265	1097	22	3.3	6	12	0.8
425	1783	23	5.7	6	52	2.9
406	1702	24	5.7	8	43	6.4
178	740	13	4.4	6	10	0.5
228	947	18	6.8	6	11	0.5
196	815	14	5.7	5	13	0.5
349	1455	21	8.3	12	30	1.7
337	1408	21	8.3	13	25	3.8
277	1156	18	7.1	7	24	1.5
269	1121	18	7.1	8	20	3.1
440	1834	31	14.4	18	24	0.8
431	1796	31	14.6	18	20	2.7
396	1655	26	10.8	15	26	1.3
388	1616	27	10.8	16	22	3.1
480	2005	33	16	18	28	1.4
472	1966	34	16.1	19	25	3.1
398	1659	27	12.2	14	26	1.3

PASTRY DISHES	AVERAGE PORTION g	GI	GL
Quiche, mushroom, wholemeal	140	L	M
Quiche, spinach	140	L	M
Quiche, spinach, wholemeal	140	L	M
Quiche, vegetable	140	L	M
Quiche, vegetable, wholemeal	140	L	M
Sausage rolls, flaky pastry	60	M	M
Sausage rolls, shortcrust pastry	60	M	M
Steak and kidney pie, double crust	120	M	M
Steak and kidney pie, shop bought	141	M	M

Unless otherwise specified, all pastry dishes are homemade.

ENERGY kcal	ENERGY kJ	FAT g	SATURATED FAT g	PROTEIN g	CARBO- HYDRATE g	FIBRE g
388	1618	28	12.2	15	21	3.1
287	1203	18	5.6	14	18	2
281	1176	18	5.6	15	16	3.2
295	1238	18	6	7	28	2.1
286	1197	18	6	8	24	3.9
238	991	17	6.5	6	15	0.8
229	953	16	5.8	6	17	0.9
406	1694	26	9.7	16	27	1.1
437	1826	24	11.8	12	38	0.7

MILK-BASED PUDDINGS & DESSERTS	AVERAGE PORTION g	GI	GL
Blancmange	150	L	L
Fruit fool	120	L	L
Fruit fool, low-fat	120	L	L
Milk pudding, made with semi-skimmed milk	200	L	L
Milk pudding, made with whole milk	200	L	L
Rice desserts, individual, with fruit	135	M	H
Rice pudding, canned	200	M	H
Tiramisu	90	L	M
Trifle, chocolate	113	M	M
Trifle, fruit	113	M	M

CHEESECAKES			
Chocolate	120	H	H
Frozen	90	H	H
Fruit, individual	90	H	H
Fruit, large	120	H	H

OTHER DESSERTS			
Christmas pudding	100	H	H
Crumble, fruit	170	H	H
Jelly, made with water	115	L	L
Pancakes	77	H	H
Pavlova, chocolate	100	H	H
Pavlova, fruit	100	H	H
Profiteroles with chocolate sauce	155	H	H
Strudel, fruit	115	H	H

MOUSSE			
Chocolate, individual	60	L	M
Chocolate	60	L	M
Fruit	60	L	M

ENERGY kcal	ENERGY kJ	FAT g	SATURATED FAT g	PROTEIN g	CARBOHYDRATE g	FIBRE g
171	720	6	3.4	5	27	Trace
213	890	13	8.8	3	22	0.5
97	405	6	0.0	4	8	0.5l
214	914	4	2.2	8	40	0.2
258	1086	9	5.4	8	40	0.2
153	648	3	2.0	4	29	0.4
178	748	3	3.2	7	28	0.4
220	919	13	7.7	4	24	0.4
233	971	17	10.7	5	15	1.4
161	672	10	6.3	3	15	2.4
415	1731	28	14.4	6	37	0.8
218	915	10	5	5	30	0.8
238	1000	11	6.8	5	31	0.9
353	1477	19	11.8	5	42	1.0
291	1227	10	4.5	5	50	1.3
373	1571	14	6.7	4	61	2.2
70	299	0	0	1	17	0
149	625	2	0.4	4	28.3	Trace
370	1552	20	10.7	4	47	0.3
288	1210	13	7.1	3	42	0.3
535	2226	40	21.7	9	38	1.1
279	1167	16	6.0	3	33	1.2
83	352	4	2.7	2	12	0.1
73	310	2	1.5	3	11	0.1
82	345	3	2	3	11	0.1

PIES	AVERAGE PORTION g	GI	GL
Apple pie, deep filled, double crust	110	M	M
Apple pie, double crust	110	M	M
Banoffee pie	150	H	M
Lemon meringue pie	150	M	M
Mince pies, individual	55	H	M
Mississippi mud pie	150	M	M

ICE CREAM AND FROZEN DESSERTS			
Arctic roll	50	M	M
Banana split	100	M	M
Chocolate-covered ice cream bar	51	M	M
Chocolate nut sundae	60	M	M
Frozen ice cream dessert, chocolate	60	M	M
Frozen ice cream dessert, plain	60	M	M
Ice cream, chocolate	75	M	L
Ice cream, dairy-free	75	L	L
Ice cream, fruit	75	L	L
Ice cream, luxury, vanilla	75	L	L
Ice cream, soya	75	L	L
Ice cream, vanilla	75	L	L
Ice cream, virtually fat free	75	L	L
Ice cream bar, chocolate flavoured coating	48	L	L
Ice cream cone, chocolate/mint/nuts	73	M	M
Ice cream cone, strawberry	81	M	M
Knickerbocker glory	100	M	M
Kulfi	80	M	M
Lolly, fruit	73	L	M
Lolly, ice cream, with fruit coating	73	L	L
Peach melba	60	L	M
Sorbet, fruit	75	L	M

ENERGY kcal	ENERGY kJ	FAT g	SATURATED FAT g	PROTEIN g	CARBO-HYDRATE g	FIBRE g
281	1183	12	3.8	4	42	1.1
269	1129	14	4.5	4	33	1.1
478	1997	30	15.0	6	49	3.8
377	1590	13	4.6	4	65	0.7
233	975	11	4.1	2	32	1.2
478	1997	30	15.0	6	49	3.8

100	424	3	1.5	2	17	Trace
182	761	11	6	2	19	0.6
163	679	2	7.7	3	12	0
167	699	9	5	2	21	0.1
150	627	11	8.5	2	13	0.0
136	568	9	6.7	2	14	Trace
156	653	8	5.2	3	19	0.0
156	654	9	2.8	2	17	0.1
119	499	5	3.4	2	17	0.2
161	670	11	6.8	3	13	0.0
156	654	9	2.8	2	17	0.1
115	480	6	3.6	2	14	0.0
76	324	1	Trace	3	15	0.0

142	590	10	8.8	2	11	0.0
207	867	13	9.6	3	21	0.2
201	844	10	7.1	3	28	0.2
112	473	5	2.9	2	16	0.2
339	1405	32	18.2	4	9	0.5
56	234	1	0.1	0	14	0.1
78	326	2	1	1	15	0.1
98	411	6	3.8	1	10	0.2
98	422	Trace	Trace	1	26	0

CONFECTIONERY	AVERAGE PORTION g	GI	GL
Boiled sweets	7	H	H
Bounty® bar	57	H	H
Chewy sweets	3	H	H
Chocolate, cooking	50	L	M
Chocolate, diabetic	50	L	M
Chocolate, fancy and filled	8	M	H
Chocolate, milk	54	L	M
Chocolate, plain	50	L	M
Chocolate, white	50	L	M
Chocolate-covered bar with fruit/nut	34	M	H
Chocolate-covered bar with wafer/biscuit	34	M	H
Chocolate-covered biscuit fingers	28	M	H
Chocolate-covered caramels	5	M	H
Chocolate-covered peanuts	50	L	L
Chocolate-covered wafer biscuits	22	M	H
Creme eggs®	39	M	H
Fruit gums/jellies	2	H	H
Fudge	11	H	H
Jelly beans (10)	11	H	H
Liquorice allsorts	7	H	H
Mars® bar	65	M	H
Marshmallows	5	H	H
Milky Way®	26	L	M
Nougat	70	H	H
Pastilles	3	H	H
Peanut brittle	58	L	M
Peppermint creams	6	H	H
Peppermints	6	H	H
Sherbert sweets	5	H	H
Smartie®-type sweets	15	L	M
Toffees, mixed	8	H	H
Truffles, rum	7	L	M
Turkish delight, with nuts	15	H	H
Turkish delight, without nuts	15	H	H

ENERGY kcal	ENERGY kJ	FAT g	SATURATED FAT g	PROTEIN g	CARBO-HYDRATE g	FIBRE g
23	98	Trace	0	Trace	6	0
270	1129	15	12.1	3	33	1.4
11	48	1	0.1	0	3	0
275	1147	17	14	2	29	0.6
224	934	15	9.1	5	19	0.6
36	150	2	0.9	0	5	0.1
281	1176	17	9.9	4	31	0.4
255	1069	14	8.4	3	32	1.3
265	1106	15	9.2	4	29	0
170	711	9	4.6	3	20	1.3
170	711	9	4.6	3	20	1.3
134	564	7	3.4	2	18	0.3
23	98	1	0.5	0	3	0
260	1085	13.1	5.1	5.1	30.3	2
110	462	6	3.8	2	14	0.2
163	681	6	1.8	2	28	0.5
6	28	0	0	0	2	Trace
49	205	2	1	0	9	0
40	169	0	0	0	10.2	Trace
24	104	1	0.3	0	5	0.1
287	1204	12	6.5	3	43	0.7
16	70	0	0	0	4	0
103	435	4	2.2	1	16	0.2
269	1138	6	0.8	3	54	0.6
8	32	0	0	0	2	0
280	1178	11	3.1	5	43	1.2
22	95	Trace	0	0	6	Trace
24	101	0	0	0	6	0
18	76	0	0	0	5	Trace
68	288	3	1.6	1	11	0.2
34	143	1	0.8	0	5	0
36	152	2	1.4	0	3	0.1
52	219	0	0	1	12	0
44	189	0	0	0	12	0

	AVERAGE PORTION g	GI	GL
COLD BEVERAGES			
CARBONATED DRINKS			
Cola	160	M	H
Cola, diet	160	L	L
Ginger ale, dry	160	L	L
Ginger ale, dry, diet	160	L	L
Lemonade	160	M	H
Lemonade, diet	160	L	L
Lucozade	160	H	H
Orangeade	160	L	H
Orangeade, diet	160	L	L
Root beer	160	L	M
Soda, cream	160	M	H
Tonic water	160	L	L
FRUIT JUICES			
Apple, unsweetened	160	L	M
Carrot	160	L	L
Cranberry	250	M	M
Grape, unsweetened	160	L	M
Grapefruit, unsweetened	160	L	M
Lemon, fresh	10	L	L
Lime, fresh	10	L	L
Mango, canned	160	M	H
Orange, freshly squeezed	160	L	M
Orange, unsweetened	160	L	M
Passion fruit	160	L	M
Pineapple, unsweetened	160	L	M
Pomegranate, fresh	160	L	M
Prune	160	L	M
Tomato	160	L	L

ENERGY kcal	ENERGY kJ	FAT g	SATURATED FAT g	PROTEIN g	CARBO-HYDRATE g	FIBRE g
66	278	0	0	Trace	17	0
Trace	Trace	0	0	0	0	0
24	99	0	0	0	6	0
2	6	0	0	0	0.4	0
35	149	0	0	Trace	9	0
Trace	Trace	0	0	0	0	0
96	410	0	0	Trace	26	0
113	474	0	0	0	27	0
1	4	0	0	0	0.4	0
66	275	0	0	0	17	0
82	344	0	0	0	21	0
53	226	0	0	0	14	0
61	262	Trace	Trace	0	16	Trace
38	165	Trace	Trace	1	9	0.2
143	595	0	0	0	36	Trace
74	314	Trace	Trace	0	19	0
53	224	Trace	Trace	1	13	Trace
1	3	Trace	Trace	0	0	0
1	4	Trace	Trace	0	0	0
62	266	Trace	Trace	0	16	Trace
53	224	Trace	Trace	1	13	0.2
58	245	Trace	Trace	1	14	0.2
75	302	Trace	Trace	1	17	Trace
66	283	Trace	Trace	0	17	Trace
70	302	Trace	Trace	0	19	Trace
91	389	Trace	Trace	1	23	Trace
22	99	Trace	Trace	1	5	1

FRUIT SQUASHES & DRINKS	AVERAGE PORTION g	GI	GL
Barley water, orange/lemon flavour	250	M	M
Blackcurrant juice drink	288	M	M
Drink, citrus/apple/mixed fruit flavours	250	M	M
Drink, low-calorie, lemon/orange/ mixed fruit flavours	250	L	L
Drink, low-sugar, fortified with vitamins	250	L	L
Fruit juice drink	206	M	M
Fruit juice drink, carbonated	160	M	M
Fruit juice drink, low calorie, mixed fruit flavours	206	M	M
Glucose drinks	250	H	H
High juice drink, orange/lemon flavours	250	M	M

MILK-BASED DRINKS			
Chocolate milk drink, low fat	250	L	L
Drinking yogurt	200	L	L
Flavoured milk	214	L	L
Milkshake, with semi-skimmed milk	300	L	L
Milkshake, with skimmed milk	300	L	L
Milkshake, with whole milk	300	L	L
Milkshake syrup, with semi- skimmed milk	290	L	L
Milkshake syrup, with skimmed milk	290	L	L
Milkshake syrup, with whole milk	297	L	L
Soya milk, flavoured	146	L	L
Probiotic yoghurt drink, orange	100	L	L
Probiotic yoghurt drink, plain	100	L	L

HOT DRINKS			
Cappuccino, with semi-skimmed milk	190	H	H
Cappuccino, with skimmed milk	190	H	H
Cappuccino, with whole milk	190	H	H

ENERGY kcal	ENERGY kJ	FAT g	SATURATED FAT g	PROTEIN g	CARBO-HYDRATE g	FIBRE g
35	150	0	0	0	9	0
86	372	0	0	Trace	23	0
48	200	0	0	Trace	13	0
3	8	0	0	Trace	1	0
10	43	0	0	Trace	3	0
76	328	Trace	Trace	0	20	Trace
62	264	Trace	Trace	Trace	16	Trace
21	89	Trace	Trace	0	5	Trace
150	640	0	0	Trace	40	0
63	268	0	0	0	16	0
183	775	5	3.1	9	27.2	Trace
124	526	Trace	Trace	6	26	Trace
146	614	3	1.9	8	23	0
207	882	5	3	10	34	Trace
171	726	1	0.3	10	34	0
261	1104	11	7.2	9	33	Trace
171	725	4	2.6	8	27	0
136	576	1	0.2	9	27	0
223	936	10	6.2	8	27	0
58	245	2	0.3	4	5	Trace
67	279	0.9	0.6	1.5	13.4	1.3
68	284	1	0.7	1.7	13.1	1.4
46	193	2	1	3	5	0
33	141	0	0.1	3	5	0
65	269	4	2.3	3	5	0

HOT DRINKS

	AVERAGE PORTION g	GI	GL
Cocoa, with semi-skimmed milk	250	H	H
Cocoa, with skimmed milk	250	H	H
Cocoa, with whole milk	250	L	L
Coffee and chicory essence, with water	190	L	L
Coffee, filter	190	L	L
Coffee, filter, with semi-skimmed milk	190	L	L
Coffee, filter, with skimmed milk	190	L	L
Coffee, filter, with single cream	190	L	L
Coffee, filter, with whole milk	190	L	L
Coffee, instant	190	L	L
Coffee, instant, with semi-skimmed milk	190	L	L
Coffee, instant, with skimmed milk	190	L	L
Coffee, instant, with whole milk	190	L	L
Coffee, Irish	125	L	L
Drinking chocolate, with semi-skimmed milk	190	H	H
Drinking chocolate, with skimmed milk	190	H	H
Drinking chocolate, with whole milk	190	H	H
Latte, with semi-skimmed milk	190	L	L
Latte, with skimmed milk	190	L	L
Latte, with whole milk	190	L	L
Mocha with semi-skimmed milk	190	L	L
Mocha with skimmed milk	190	L	L
Mocha with whole milk	190	L	L
Ovaltine®, with semi-skimmed milk	190	H	H
Ovaltine®, with skimmed milk	190	H	H
Ovaltine®, with whole milk	190	H	H
Tea, black	190	L	L
Tea, Chinese	190	L	L
Tea, green	190	L	L
Tea, herbal	190	L	L
Tea, lemon, instant	190	L	L
Tea, with semi-skimmed milk	190	L	L

ENERGY kcal	ENERGY kJ	FAT g	SATURATED FAT g	PROTEIN g	CARBO-HYDRATE g	FIBRE g
143	608	5	3	9	18	0.5
110	475	1	0.8	9	18	0.5
190	800	10	6.5	9	17	0.5
17	76	Trace	0	0	5	0
4	15	Trace	Trace	0	1	0
13	55	1	0.2	1	1	0
11	43	0	0	1	1	0
27	106	2	1.3	1	1	0
13	59	1	0.6	1	1	0
Trace	4	Trace	0	0	Trace	0
13	55	1	0.2	1	1	0
8	39	0	0	1	1	0
15	65	1	0.6	1	1	0
105	433	10	6.1	1	4	0
135	578	4	2.3	7	21	Trace
112	481	1	0.6	7	21	Trace
171	716	8	4.8	6	20	Trace
60	252	2	1.3	4	7	0
33	141	1	0.1	3	5	0
85	353	5	3	4	6	0
96	405	5	3.1	4	9	0.1
81	339	3	2	4	9	0.1
120	500	7	4.8	4	9	0.1
150	642	3	1.9	7	25	Trace
129	549	1	0.2	7	25	Trace
184	779	7	4.6	7	25	Trace
Trace	4	Trace	Trace	0	Trace	0
2	10	0	0	0	0	0
Trace	Trace	0	0	0	Trace	0
2	25	Trace	Trace	0	0	0
15	65	0	0	0	4	0
13	53	1	0.2	1	1	0

HOT DRINKS	AVERAGE PORTION g	GI	GL
Tea with skimmed milk	190	L	L
Tea with whole milk	190	L	L
BEERS			
Bitter, best/premium	287	H	H
Bitter, bottled	287	H	H
Bitter, canned	287	H	H
Bitter, draught	287	H	H
Bitter, keg	287	H	H
Bitter, low-alcohol	250	H	H
Brown ale, bottled	250	H	H
Mild, draught	287	H	H
Pale ale, bottled	250	H	H
Strong ale/barley wine	287	H	H
CIDERS			
Dry	287	L	L
Low-alcohol	250	L	L
Sweet	287	H	H
Vintage	287	H	H
LAGERS			
Bottled	250	H	H
Canned	287	H	H
Draught	287	H	H
Low-alcohol	250	H	H
Premium	287	H	H
Shandy	287	H	H

ENERGY kcal	ENERGY kJ	FAT g	SATURATED FAT g	PROTEIN g	CARBO- HYDRATE g	FIBRE g
8	36	0	0	1	1	0
15	61	1	0.6	1	1	0
95	399	Trace	Trace	1	6	Trace
86	356	Trace	Trace	1	6	Trace
92	379	Trace	Trace	1	7	0
92	379	Trace	Trace	1	7	0
89	370	Trace	Trace	1	7	0
33	135	0	0	1	5	Trace
75	315	Trace	Trace	1	8	Trace
69	293	Trace	Trace	1	5	Trace
70	295	Trace	Trace	1	5	Trace
189	789	Trace	Trace	2	18	Trace
103	436	0	0	Trace	7	0
43	185	0	0	Trace	9	0
121	505	0	0	Trace	12	0
290	1208	0	0	Trace	21	0
73	300	Trace	Trace	1	4	0
83	347	Trace	Trace	1	Trace	Trace
83	347	Trace	Trace	1	Trace	Trace
25	103	Trace	Trace	1	4	Trace
169	700	Trace	Trace	1	7	Trace
32	138	0	0	Trace	9	Trace

LIQUEURS

	AVERAGE PORTION g	GI	GL
Advocaat	25	M	M
Cherry Brandy	25	H	H
Coîntreau	25	H	H
Cream liqueurs	25	H	H
Crème de Menthe	25	H	H
Curaçao	25	H	H
Drambuie	25	H	H
Egg nog	160	H	H
Grand Marnier	25	H	H
Pernod	25	H	H
Southern Comfort	25	H	H
Tia Maria	25	H	H

FORTIFIED WINES

Port	50	L	L
Sherry, dry	50	L	L
Sherry, medium	50	L	L
Sherry, sweet	50	L	L
Tonic wine	125	L	L
Vermouth, dry	48	L	L
Vermouth, sweet	48	L	L

SPIRITS, 40% VOLUME

Brandy	25	L	L
Gin	25	L	L
Rum	25	L	L
Vodka	25	L	L
Whisky	25	L	L

ENERGY kcal	ENERGY kJ	FAT g	SATURATED FAT g	PROTEIN g	CARBO-HYDRATE g	FIBRE g
65	273	2	0.5	1	7	0
66	275	0	0	Trace	8	0
79	328	0	0	Trace	6	0
81	338	4	0	Trace	6	0
66	275	0	0	Trace	8	0
78	326	0	0	Trace	7	0
79	328	0	0	Trace	6	0
182	763	7	3.4	6	16	0
79	328	0	0	Trace	6	0
79	328	0	0	Trace	6	0
79	328	0	0	Trace	6	0
66	275	0	0	Trace	8	0
79	328	0	0	0	6	0
58	241	0	0	0	1	0
58	241	0	0	0	3	0
68	284	0	0	0	3	0
159	665	0	0	Trace	15	0
52	217	0	0	0	1	0
72	303	0	0	Trace	8	0
52	215	0	0	Trace	Trace	0
52	215	0	0	Trace	Trace	0
52	215	0	0	Trace	Trace	0
52	215	0	0	Trace	Trace	0
52	215	0	0	Trace	Trace	0

STOUT	AVERAGE PORTION g	GI	GL
Bottled	250	H	H
Extra	287	H	H
Guinness™	287	H	H
Mackeson	287	H	H
WINES			
Champagne	125	L	L
Mulled wine	125	L	L
Red wine	125	L	L
Rosé, medium	125	L	L
White wine, dry	125	L	L
White wine, medium	125	L	L
White wine, sparkling	125	L	L
White wine, sweet	125	L	L

ENERGY kcal	ENERGY kJ	FAT g	SATURATED FAT g	PROTEIN g	CARBO-HYDRATE g	FIBRE g
93	390	Trace	Trace	1	10	0
112	468	Trace	Trace	1	6	0
86	362	Trace	Trace	1	4	0
103	439	Trace	Trace	1	13	0
95	394	0	0	0	2	0
245	1028	0	0	0	32	0
85	354	0	0	0	0	0
89	368	0	0	0	3	0
83	344	0	0	0	1	0
93	385	0	0	0	4	0
93	384	0	0	0	6	0
118	493	0	0	0	7	0

Special Photography
© **Octopus Publishing Group Limited**/Gareth Sambidge.

Other Photography
© **Octopus Publishing Group Limited**/Ian O'Leary 8–15, 16–33, 80–85, 86–93, 130–131, 132–143.

Commissioning Editor Nicola Hill
Managing Editor Clare Churly
Design Manager Tokiko Morishima
Designer Peter Gerrish
Picture Librarian Sophie Delpech
Production Assistant Nosheen Shan